EXAM *Revision* NOTES

AS Law

Emma Bradbury

Caroline Rowlands

2nd Edition

Philip Allan Updates, an imprint of Hodder Education, part of Hachette Livre UK, Market Place, Deddington, Oxfordshire OX15 0SE

Orders

2 006 002 317

Bookpoint Ltd, 130 Milton Park, Abingdon, Oxfordshire, OX14 4SB
tel: 01235 827720
fax: 01235 400454
e-mail: uk.orders@bookpoint.co.uk
Lines are open 9.00 a.m.–5.00 p.m., Monday to Saturday, with a 24-hour message answering service. You can also order through the Philip Allan Updates website: www.philipallan.co.uk

ISBN: 978-1-84489-505-2

Printed in Spain

Hachette Livre UK's policy is to use papers that are natural, renewable and recyclable products and made from wood grown in sustainable forests. The logging and manufacturing processes are expected to conform to the environmental regulations of the country of origin.

Contents

Introduction

Authors

Emma Bradbury and **Caroline Rowlands** are both teachers at Aquinas College in Stockport, Cheshire. They have experience of teaching GCSE Law, AQA and OCR AS and A2 Law, and law access courses. Emma has an LLB (Hons) and a Masters degree in Law and Medicine. Caroline has completed a BA (Hons), the Common Professional Examination and the Bar Vocational Course.

About this book

How to use the book

This book has been written to help AQA and OCR Law students prepare for their AS examinations. The topics included cover both specifications, but make sure you know whether you are following an AQA or an OCR course, and get a copy of the specification if you are not sure. Your teacher may have provided you with a specification at the beginning of the course but if in doubt, they can be found on the exam boards' websites.

Structure

There are 19 topics, which are split into headings marked A, B, C etc. Each heading is then split into sections numbered 1, 2, 3 etc. There are further subsections numbered 1.1, 1.2, 1.3 etc. The structure of the topics is designed to help you revise an area of law in small sections, yet still be able to see how it fits into the topic as a whole.

Topic summaries

The summaries at the end of each topic are a good way to remind yourself of the main points, but remember that it is the details that get you the best marks in an exam.

Tips

Tips are included in the margin. These include definitions, exam advice and extra information to aid your understanding.

Cases

As law students, you will come across a vast number of cases. It is neither necessary nor feasible for you to remember them all. We have tried to include the best-known cases as well as some recent ones. If your teacher has given you a different case to use as an example then use whichever case you understand and can remember best. An examiner does not want you to memorise a list of cases. It is much better to know a few cases with some detail than a lot of cases with no detail. Cases are used to explain a point that you are making in the exam.

Preparation for exams

Exam preparation should not take place in the couple of weeks before the exam. Checking your notes are correct, organising your file and writing revision notes can all be done well in advance. Once you finish a module or even one topic in a module, there is no reason not to make exam preparations while the information is fresh in your mind. There is a big difference between preparing for exams and the actual revision that you do to memorise the information. The more preparation that you do in advance, the more time you will have to revise thoroughly in the weeks leading up to the exam.

Up-to-date notes

It is always a good idea to check that your notes are accurate and up to date. It is possible that you misheard something in a lesson or wrote something down that is incorrect. It is essential that your notes are correct and that you understand them. The best way to check your notes and improve your understanding is to read a textbook. You may have one that you use for the course, or else you can borrow one from the library. It is sometimes helpful to read other textbooks as they give you a different explanation that you may understand better. If you are absent from a lesson it is up to you to make sure that you copy up and make sure you understand what you have missed. If you are already on study leave it is too late to find you have gaps in your notes or you do not understand something.

Organising your file

Organising your file is another ongoing process. By taking a few minutes every week you can make sure that your notes are filed in the correct order and that you are only carrying around what you need for each lesson. One idea is to take out of the file the notes for each topic as you complete them. Either put them in a separate file at home (one for each module) or hold each topic together with a treasury tag. Make a title page for each topic, including which module it is for and a list of its contents.

Reading textbooks and articles

Reading is very important in the study of law. When you finish a topic in class, read the chapter in the textbook to improve your understanding. You can also read chapters in advance if you know what topic you are about to learn in your lessons. If you find an important quotation or example, write it down and put it with your notes.

There are some excellent law journals available. Find out if your library subscribes to any of them, and, if not, subscribe yourself. They include regular updates of new cases and changes in the law.

If your teacher gives you newspaper articles, information from the internet or reports from law journals, make sure that you write down the important points and add these to your notes. It is extremely difficult to revise from a textbook or long article, so you need to pick out the important parts.

Understanding

If you do not understand something that you do in class or read in a textbook, it is vital that you ask someone for help. This could be asking one of your classmates to explain it to you in his or her own words, or seeing your teacher after class. It is difficult to learn something and write about it in an exam if you do not really understand it. It is obvious

to an examiner when you have simply memorised information. Do not wait until just before the exam to ask for help. Do it while the topic is still fresh in your mind. Above all, take responsibility for your own learning.

Making revision notes

Revision notes can be made well in advance. It is difficult to revise from lengthy notes, so you need to make concise points that trigger your memory. Use your full class notes and the textbooks to learn the law and then use short revision notes to remind you of the main points.

Revision notes should be clear. Try to keep to one piece of A4 paper per topic. This may mean writing small, but revision notes should not simply be a copy of your class notes. Use different-coloured pens and a clear format, e.g. cases written in red pen, statutes written in green pen. This will make the notes stand out. Writing things down is a good way to memorise information — much better that simply reading it.

Revision notes should be concise. Use abbreviations and only write down the minimum amount of information that is necessary to trigger your memory. For example, if you were making a revision note on Private Member's Bills and wanted to remember the example of the abolition of the death penalty which was sponsored by Sydney Silverman and led to the **Murder Act 1965**, it would be easier to write:

PMB Syd Silverman Murder Act 65

Revision notes can take many forms. They can be written as a spider diagram, a table, a flow diagram or whichever way you find easiest to learn.

Planning for exams

Timetable

It is essential to organise your time in the run-up to the exams:

- You need to decide how much time to allocate to revising each topic. This will help you work out how much time you need and when you should start your revision programme in the run-up to the exams. If you are taking exams in June, the Easter holidays are the best time to start.
- You should allocate yourself time each day for revising.
- Make a timetable that includes time for study as well as other activities that you do.
- Stick to the timetable. If something comes up you need to reallocate the revision you were going to do to another time.
- Keep the sessions short, e.g. 45 minutes, and take breaks. Alternate the subjects that you are revising in a day so you do not get bogged down with too much law.
- If you want to give yourself the best chance in the exams, make sure that you give yourself ample time to revise.

The exam

Make sure you find out the exact dates and times of the exams that you are taking. It may be that you are taking two or even three exams one after the other. Always double-check to make sure you know whether exams are in the morning or afternoon. Try to find out in advance which room the exam is going to be held in.

It is also important that you know the format of the exam. Look at past papers so that you know how many questions to answer and how much time to allocate to each question.

Revision

Past papers

Past exam papers are an excellent way to prepare for the sorts of questions that you will face in the exam. The exam papers offer you a choice of question. Make sure that you would be able to answer the appropriate number of questions on each past paper. There may be topics in a module that you would prefer to answer in an exam, but it is extremely risky to try to 'question-spot'. You may have some favourite topics, but make sure you could answer other questions as well, in case your favourites are not there.

Your teacher should be able to provide you with past papers but you can also get them from the exam board website. Another useful thing is to look at the mark schemes and examiner's report (also available on the internet). The mark scheme lists the potential content that the examiner is expecting for each question on the exam paper. You can compare what you think you would write for a question with what the examiner is expecting to see. The examiner's report is written by the chief examiner and contains his/her overall view of the exam. He/she will remark on where the candidates had weaknesses and which questions were answered well.

Techniques

There are lots of methods of revising and you may already know what works best for you. It can also be worth trying other techniques. Using different-coloured pens to make your revision notes stand out is mentioned above, as is the use of diagrams. You may wish to use coloured highlighters in this book to mark the important parts.

When it comes to remembering cases, you can either keep testing yourself until the information reaches your long-term memory or you can try other techniques. Try to associate the name of the case and what happened as a picture. It could even be a scene. A silly image is often easier to remember. For example, imagine a fisherman wearing a parka coat. He has a bell and a knife on the end of his fishing line. Do you get it? The picture is describing the statutory interpretation case of *Fisher* v *Bell*, which involved a flick knife being displayed in a shop window. The judge who decided the case was Lord Parker.

Another excellent way of remembering the order of something is to take the first letter of each point and make up a different sentence. This is regularly used when trying to learn trigonometry at school. The following example, which describes the parliamentary stage of the legislation process, has been tried and tested by all of our students over the years:

The parliamentary stage is made up of seven main stages: first reading, second reading, committee stage, report stage, third reading, House of Lords, royal assent.

Take the first letter of each stage: F S C R T H R

Remember the order of the letters with this rhyme: Fat Snails Can't Reach The Hand Rails.

Some students learn best by reading out loud or hearing their notes spoken. This is called auditory learning. If you like this kind of learning, then read from your notes or revise with

one of your classmates and explain different points to each other. You could even tape your voice and listen to it on your way to the exam.

Testing yourself

In order to commit things to memory it is necessary to keep testing yourself. The repetition helps you learn facts and figures. There are a number of ways to do this. Getting someone to test you is always a good idea, but try to do this with one of your classmates as it can often lead to arguments when you ask a parent.

An excellent way to test yourself is by reading through your revision notes and then trying to write down the main points. It may be that you can only remember a few the first time you do it, but with practice you will remember more and more. The more you test yourself, the more you will remember.

Timed questions

Many students run out of time in the exam, so you need to be aware of how long you can spend on each question. Practise exam technique by writing timed answers to past papers. Another useful exercise is to put your notes away and try to write down as much as you can remember about a topic in 10 minutes. After 10 minutes, look back at your notes to see what you have missed. The more you do this, the more you will remember each time.

The night before

Many people say that you should not revise the night before an exam. We agree that you should not still be writing revision notes the night before, but you can always test yourself and read through your notes.

Double-check the time of the exam and prepare the equipment you will need. Your pencil case must be see-through but if you have not got one, just take your pens loose. The exam should be written in blue or black ink (e.g. a biro) so take a few in case one runs out.

Exam techniques

In the exam room

Remember that mobile phones must be switched off and must not be in your pocket or anywhere near your desk. If you have a phone with you, give it to the invigilator to look after.

Get to the exam room early so that you can find your seat number and get settled. Read the instructions on the exam paper carefully.

Plans

Before you start to answer the questions, read through the whole paper. It is worth writing a quick plan of your answer so that you structure it well and you do not forget to include important information. There is no need to cross out a plan, as the examiner may like to see it.

Timing

You must be very strict with yourself as regards how long you spend on each question. Find out in advance how long you can spend on a question worth a certain amount of

marks in the exam, e.g. if you have to answer three 20-mark questions in 1 hour, you have 20 minutes to answer each question.

Your own opinion

Most exams do not require you to give your own opinion, so it is best avoided. Starting sentences with 'I think...' is not appropriate. It is likely that a judge or legal academic has already thought it before you, so it would be best to quote them instead. If you do not know who made a certain point, then start your sentence in a more general manner, e.g. 'It has also been remarked...' or 'Some may argue...'.

Answer the question

This may seem obvious but examiners constantly complain about candidates not answering the question. Students see a question on the exam paper and try to write everything they know in the hope that some of it will be appropriate. This is not what the examiners want. Make sure you read the question carefully and underline the important parts. An example of an exam question could be:

Describe the selection of juries and the role they play in criminal cases.

The important parts of the question are:

Describe the *selection* of juries and the *role* they play in *criminal* cases.

The word 'describe' indicates that this question requires an explanation of the law with no need for evaluation. The question is asking you to do two things: explain the selection (how juries are chosen) and their role (what they have to do in a case). A very important part of this question is that it specifies 'criminal cases' only. You will not receive marks for writing about a jury's role in a civil case, nor will you get marks for discussing the advantages and disadvantages of juries.

By making reference to the words used in the question throughout your answer, you are showing the examiner that you are answering the actual question and not the one that you hoped would come up.

Use examples

Students who do well in law exams are able to include examples in their answers. This could be an Act of Parliament that created a law, a statistic, a quotation by a judge, a criticism made by the Law Commission or legal academic, or a case that illustrates a point of law. Always try to use examples in your answers but do not just list cases. It is usually necessary to give a bit of detail about the facts of a case, or the law that it established, in order to illustrate a point.

Write in continuous prose

Answers to exam questions should be written as an essay with a proper structure and a conclusion. This is difficult in the time constraints of the exam but you should try to avoid lists, bullet points and diagrams if you can. Short-answer questions should always be answered in full sentences.

GOOD LUCK!

For more information
about the work
of Parliament visit
www.parliament.uk

Legislation is the process by which Parliament makes laws. Parliament is made up of the House of Commons, the House of Lords and the monarch, and all three have a role in the legislation process. The House of Commons is the elected chamber in Parliament and comprises Members of Parliament (MPs) who are members of the government and the opposition parties. There is also a speaker who controls the proceedings in the House of Commons. The government controls the legislative agenda. The House of Lords is the second chamber in Parliament. It consists of unelected peers, Law Lords (judges) and bishops.

A Types of bill

An idea for a new Act of Parliament starts its journey through the legislation process as a bill. There are three types of bill: public bills, private bills and private members' bills.

1 Public bills

Public bills affect the whole country and are mostly proposed by the government; consequently, they are sometimes referred to as 'government bills'. The government controls the legislative agenda, which means that it allocates the most time in Parliament to passing its own ideas for new laws. The government may get ideas for new laws from many different sources, e.g. manifesto promises that it made during its election campaign; cabinet ministers, who may propose changes to the laws concerning their department; public protest and pressure groups; or official law reform organisations such as judicial inquiries, the Law Commission and Royal Commission reports.

Each political party produces a manifesto in the run-up to a general election.

These bills are most likely to complete the legislation process and become law as the government has a majority in the House of Commons.

The Labour government won the 2005 general election with a majority of 66 MPs.

2 Private bills

Private bills may be introduced to Parliament by a large company, a local council or a public corporation when it requires an Act of Parliament to build a new road or factory, for example. These bills do not usually affect the whole country.

3 Private members' bills

Private members' bills usually have a 'free vote' where the MPs can vote according to their own opinion.

These are bills put forward by backbench MPs from any of the political parties. The MP puts his or her name into a ballot at the beginning of the year and 20 names are drawn out. These MPs are then allocated time to explain their bill to the rest of the House. The Ten-Minute Rule does not give them much time to do this and there must be enough MPs in attendance for the vote to be counted. During the 10 minutes other MPs may waste time through false argument. This is known as filibustering. It is not surprising that private members' bills are usually unsuccessful, as they do not have the support of their party. For example, David Alton put forward many unsuccessful private members' bills to change the abortion laws.

Private members' bills are a good way of raising awareness of a controversial issue that the government might not wish to commit itself to. An example of a successful private members' bill was that which led to the **Murder (Abolition of the Death Penalty) Act 1965**, which was proposed by Sydney Silverman, a Labour backbench MP.

Another successful private members' bill was proposed by Doug Hoyle, who abolished the year and a day rule for the crime of murder in 1996 (**Law Reform (Year and a Day Rule) Act 1996**).

B Legislation process

The legislation process has four main stages. The most important one to learn is the parliamentary stage.

1 Idea stage

See Topic 6 for more information on this stage.

The idea for a new law can come from many different sources such as the Law Commission, Royal Commission reports, manifesto promises etc. The government devises most new laws.

2 Consultation stage

The idea is discussed with experts and interested parties and a Green Paper is formulated. This is known as a 'discussion document'. The finalised version of the idea is then produced as a White Paper, which is the government's 'statement of intent'.

3 Drafting stage

It is important that a bill is drafted properly as a badly worded law causes problems when a judge has to apply it to a case.

The idea is written into legal terminology by the Parliamentary Counsel. It has now become a bill and is ready to be presented to Parliament.

4 Parliamentary stage

The legislation process is the stages that a bill must pass through in order to become an Act of Parliament. The most important stages take place in Parliament. Parliament is made up of the House of Commons, House of Lords and the monarch. The process can start in either the House of Commons or the House of Lords (with the exception of finance bills, which must start in the House of Commons).

It is important to learn these stages in the correct order. An easy way to remember is to take the first letter of each stage (F, S, C, R, T, H, R) and create a sentence. Try: Fat Snails Can't Reach The Hand Rails.

4.1 First reading

The title of the bill is read out by the MP who is sponsoring it, e.g. the home secretary would sponsor a bill involving the power of the police. The bill is then published and a date is set for the second reading.

This is the most crucial stage for a bill to pass.

4.2 Second reading

The whole House debates the bill. If there is a division, a vote is called. The MPs vote by passing through either the 'aye' door or the 'no' door. They are then counted as they return to their seats. The speaker will announce if the 'ayes have it', which means there is a majority of votes in favour of the bill. It will then pass to the next stage. The political parties use the 'whip' system to ensure party support for an important bill.

4.3 Committee stage

The bill is now scrutinised by a group of MPs called the standing committee. These committees are usually composed of between 16 and 30 MPs, reflecting the composition of Parliament. Any suggestions made at the second reading are considered and the committee may suggest amendments, additions and deletions to the bill.

4.4 Report stage

The standing committee reports back to the House with any proposals for changes to the bill. Each change is debated by the House, which will vote on it. If there are not any proposed changes this stage does not occur.

4.5 Third reading

This is the last read-through of the bill. There may be a short debate and a vote on any final changes to be made. The bill is then said to have 'passed through the House'. It continues its journey through Parliament in the second chamber.

4.6 House of Lords

The House of Lords is made up of unelected peers. Since the **House of Lords Act 1999** there are a few remaining hereditary peers with the rest of the House comprising life peers, bishops and the Law Lords. The role of the House of Lords is to scrutinise the bill further and it may suggest amendments, which must be approved by the House of Commons. The House of Lords has the power to delay a bill for 1 year (1 month for finance bills) but it cannot prevent a bill being passed. The House of Commons may invoke the **Parliament Act** if it wishes to avoid this delay and bypass the House of Lords. This has been used seven times since 1911.

The most recent use of the **Parliament Act** was to pass the **Hunting Act 2005**.

4.7 Royal assent

The bill becomes an Act of Parliament once the Queen signs it, giving it her royal assent.

C Evaluation

There are many advantages and disadvantages of the legislation process. Some are specific to a particular stage in the process and some are general criticisms of the whole process.

1 Advantages

- The process ensures that it takes a long time for a bill to become an Act of Parliament. This enables the bill to be effectively scrutinised and checked for errors.
- The first reading allows the opposition to obtain a copy of the bill and prepare its arguments for the debate at the second reading.
- The whips ensure that MPs vote with their party. The public vote for an MP to represent them in Parliament and choose them according to the party they support. An MP should therefore agree with his or her party's policies, even if he or she personally disagrees.
- The standing committee scrutinises the bill, looking for errors and suggesting changes.
- The House of Lords contains many experts including ex-politicians, medical professionals and business people. They act as a 'safety net' in that they often find errors that the House of Commons has missed.
- Acts of Parliament receive a royal crest and it gives the monarch a role in Parliament.
- Private members' bills allow backbench MPs and members of the opposition to create laws that the government has not timetabled.

> The House of Lords restricts the government's powers but it cannot prevent a bill from becoming law.

2 Disadvantages

- The lengthy process means that some bills run out of time and have to be reintroduced in the next Parliament or not at all. Some bills are rushed through the process and are passed containing errors, e.g. the **Dangerous Dogs Act 1991**.
- Professor Zander called the first reading 'a pure moment of nothing'. It can appear a waste of time.
- The whips system is seen as undemocratic and the whips have been accused of 'bully' tactics.
- The standing committee will always have a majority of government MPs sitting on it, so it may control what changes are suggested.
- The House of Lords is unelected and therefore undemocratic.
- The role of the Queen in the legislation process is no more than tradition. She cannot refuse to sign a bill and often one of her staff will sign it on her behalf. This stage has been called a 'rubber-stamping exercise'.
- The ballot restricts the number of private members' bills that can be considered (only 20 per year). The Ten-Minute Rule prevents most of the MPs from getting a proper chance to explain their idea, and other MPs will waste this time by filibustering (wasting time through false argument).

> The government is currently considering whether the Lords should be selected or elected.

D Supremacy of Parliament

Parliament is the supreme lawmaker in the UK. Statutory laws must be applied by the courts and take precedence over any existing common law (judge-made law).

Since the **Human Rights Act 1998** came into force, new Acts of Parliament should be compatible with it but will still be applied by the courts even if they are not. Parliament can pass laws that are not compatible with the **Human Rights Act** if it has taken the Act into account when passing the law. Section 19 of the **Human Rights Act** requires that all new Acts of Parliament must state that they are compatible with human rights. If the new Act is not compatible, s.19 requires Parliament to state that this was its intention. Section 3 of the Human Rights Act requires judges to interpret the law in the light of this Act. If the judge believes that an Act is not compatible with human rights, he or she can make a declaration of incompatibility suggesting that Parliament should make an amendment. A judge cannot refuse to follow an Act of Parliament even if it contravenes the Human Rights Act.

The UK joined the European Union in 1973 and so must adhere to the **European Communities Act 1972**, which states that the EU laws take precedence over UK statutes. Parliament is therefore no longer sovereign over EU matters, although the UK could withdraw from the EU if it so wished. Parliament devolved some power to Scotland, Wales and Northern Ireland in 1998 but it remains sovereign.

Summary of Topic 1

Legislation is the process by which Parliament makes laws. Parliament is made up of the House of Commons, the House of Lords and the monarch, and all three have a role in the legislation process.

Types of bill

There are three types:

1 **Public bills:** these affect the whole country and are proposed by the government. The government controls the legislative agenda, which means that it allocates the most time in Parliament to passing its own ideas for new laws.
2 **Private bills:** these may be introduced to Parliament by a large company, a local council or a public corporation when it requires an Act of Parliament to build a new road or factory, for example. These bills do not usually affect the whole country.
3 **Private members' bills:** these are bills put forward by backbench MPs from any of the political parties. The MP puts his or her name into a ballot at the beginning of the year and 20 names are drawn out. These MPs are then allocated time to explain their bill to the rest of the House. An example of a successful private members' bill was that which led to the **Murder (Abolition of the Death Penalty) Act 1965**, which was proposed by Sydney Silverman, a Labour backbench MP.

Legislation process

1 **Idea stage:** the idea for a new law can come from many different sources such as the Law Commission, Royal Commission reports, manifesto promises etc. The government devises most new laws.
2 **Consultation stage:** the idea is discussed with experts and interested parties and a Green Paper is formulated. This is known as a 'discussion document'. The finalised version of the idea is then produced as a White Paper, which is the government's 'statement of intent'.

3 **Drafting stage:** the idea is written into legal terminology by the Parliamentary Counsel. It has now become a bill and is ready to be presented to Parliament.

4 **Parliamentary stage:** the legislation process is the stages that a bill must pass in order to become an Act of Parliament. The most important stages take place in Parliament. The process can start in either the House of Commons or the House of Lords.

First reading: the title of the bill is read out.

Second reading: the whole House debates the bill. If there is a division, a vote will be called.

Committee stage: the bill is now scrutinised by a group of MPs called the standing committee.

Report stage: the standing committee reports back to the House with any proposals for changes to the bill.

Third reading: this is the last read-through of the bill. There may be a short debate and a vote on any final changes to be made.

House of Lords: its role is to scrutinise the bill further and it may suggest amendments, which must be approved by the House of Commons. The House of Lords has the power to delay a bill for 1 year (1 month for finance bills) but it cannot prevent a bill being passed.

Royal assent: the bill becomes an Act of Parliament once the Queen signs it, giving it her royal assent.

Supremacy of Parliament

Parliament is the supreme lawmaker in the UK. Statutory laws must be applied by the courts and take precedence over any existing common law (judge-made law). Since the **Human Rights Act 1998** came into force, new Acts of Parliament should be compatible with it but will still be applied by the courts even if they are not. The UK joined the European Union in 1973 and so must adhere to the **European Communities Act 1972**, which states that the EU laws take precedence over UK statutes. Parliament devolved some power to Scotland, Wales and Northern Ireland in 1998 but it remains sovereign.

Parliament does not have the time or expertise to pass every law that is needed each year. It is therefore necessary for it to give some of its power to other people and organisations to make laws. It gives this power in an enabling Act.

An enabling Act is sometimes known as a parent Act.

A Types of delegated legislation

1 Bylaws

These are made by local councils and other public bodies. For example, local councils may wish to ban drinking in their town centre, as occurred in Manchester in time for the Commonwealth Games. Another example would be the fines incurred by people who let their dogs foul in public parks.

Public corporations such as the buses and train services are able to impose fines for non-payment of fares.

It is important to know which of the three types of delegated legislation would be most appropriate to pass a new law.

2 Statutory instruments

These are regulations made by government departments to implement the provisions made in Acts of Parliament. For example, the **Dangerous Dogs Act 1991** allows the home secretary to add more breeds of dangerous dogs to the Act if it is deemed necessary. The Department of Constitutional Affairs can make changes to the provision of legal aid under the **Legal Aid Act 1998**. The Department of Agriculture was able to close public footpaths during the foot and mouth outbreak in 2001.

3 Orders in Council

These are laws passed by the Privy Council, which is a group of senior politicians who are allowed to make law without the need for the whole of Parliament to be sitting. They have the power to pass laws in times of emergency, with the permission of the Queen, under the **Emergency Powers Act 1920**. They may do this in wartime.

B Controls on delegated legislation

It is important that delegated legislation is checked by Parliament and can be challenged in the courts by the public.

1 General supervision of delegated legislation

1.1 Enabling Act

The enabling Act itself sets out the powers that Parliament wishes to give.

1.2 Consultation

The enabling Act may specify that certain organisations or experts must be consulted before delegated legislation is made.

1.3 Publication

All delegated legislation is published and is available for interested parties to read.

Parliamentary supervision of delegated legislation

2.1 Relevant government minister

All bylaws are checked by the relevant government minister. For example, if a council wishes to impose traffic restrictions it will be checked by the transport minister.

2.2 Joint select committees

All statutory instruments are scrutinised by a group of MPs known as a select committee. They check the provisions of any laws made and can question the minister and his or her civil servants.

2.3 Affirmative resolution procedure

Enabling Acts that give important or constitutional powers may require Parliament to vote before the delegated legislation can be passed.

Describing these procedures accurately in an exam question on controls of delegated legislation will get you extra marks.

2.4 Negative resolution procedure

Parliament may cancel a piece of delegated legislation within 40 days if an MP puts forward a motion to annul.

2.5 Question time

MPs may question ministers about a piece of delegated legislation.

Court supervision of delegated legislation

3.1 Judicial review

An organisation or member of the public may challenge a piece of delegated legislation in the High Court. The judge will interpret the wording of the enabling Act to decide if the law was made *ultra vires* (beyond the powers granted by Parliament) and if he or she finds that the legislation is *ultra vires* it will be declared void.

Always give a definition of Latin terms.

Under the Civil Procedure Rules 1999, an application for judicial review must be made within 3 months. The person making the application must also have a legal interest (*locus standi*) in the outcome of the case. This legal interest was extended to include pressure groups in *R* v *Her Majesty's Inspectorate of Pollution ex parte Greenpeace* (1994).

There are two types of *ultra vires* — substantive and procedural.

3.2 **Substantive** *ultra vires*

Delegated legislation may be declared void if it allows something that the enabling Act did not intend, e.g. in *Commissioners of Customs and Excise* v *Cure and Deeley* (1962).

> *Commissioners of Customs and Excise* v *Cure and Deeley* (1962)
> The **Finance (No. 2) Act 1940** did not allow Customs and Excise to charge extra for late tax returns so when they started to fine people they were challenged in the courts. The judge found that they had acted beyond their power and therefore it was void.

It is important to use cases to explain the two types of *ultra vires*.

> *R (Ann Summers Ltd)* v *Jobcentre Plus* (2003)
> The Job Centre refused to advertise job vacancies for Ann Summers Ltd, which is a chain of sex shops. It did this because it thought it would not be fair to force someone to work in such a shop. The judge decided that the Job Centre did not have the power to refuse to advertise jobs. He said that a person who did not want to work in a sex shop would have a good reason not to take the job.

3.3 **Procedural** *ultra vires*

The enabling Act may set out certain procedures that must be followed before delegated legislation can be passed, e.g. *Agricultural, Horticultural and Forestry Training Board* v *Aylesbury Mushrooms Ltd* (1972).

> *Agricultural, Horticultural and Forestry Training Board* v *Aylesbury Mushrooms Ltd* (1972)
> The training board was required by the enabling Act to consult anybody who might be affected by one of its laws. It did not consult the Mushroom Growers' Association and therefore the piece of delegated legislation was void.

The courts will also declare delegated legislation to be invalid when the law made under the enabling Act is 'unreasonable'. This was established in the case of *Associated Provincial Picture Houses* v *Wednesbury* (1948) and is known as 'Wednesbury unreasonableness'.

> *R* v *Sacupima ex parte Newham London Borough Council* (2000)
> This case is an example of 'Wednesbury unreasonableness'. Newham Council offered people who had become homeless bed and breakfast accommodation in Brighton. These people would not be able to afford to stay in Brighton when they had to return to Newham for their benefits, schooling and medical treatment. The decision to rehouse them so far away was held to be unreasonable.

C Evaluation

Try to keep your evaluation balanced, e.g. three advantages and three disadvantages.

1 Advantages of delegated legislation

- Delegated legislation **saves time**. Parliament is only able to pass approximately 50 Acts of Parliament per year. It is therefore vital for Parliament to delegate power to others to make the thousands of other necessary laws.
- It is **flexible**. Delegated laws can be passed much more quickly if they are not required to go through the official legislation process. This is especially advantageous when laws need to be made or changed in times of emergency.
- It is made by **experts**. Local councils are much better equipped to make bylaws concerning their area as they have the expertise to know what is best for the public in that town. Government departments are staffed by expert civil servants who understand the practicalities of making a statutory instrument better than the average MP.

2 Disadvantages of delegated legislation

- It is **undemocratic**. Civil servants who are not elected by the general public may make statutory instruments and it is therefore undemocratic for such people to have so much power to pass delegated legislation.
- The sheer **quantity** of delegated laws made every year (approximately 3,000 statutory instruments are passed each year) means that a great deal of law is being made by people and organisations that are outside of Parliament.
- **Scrutiny**: although there are numerous controls and checks available for delegated legislation, the large quantity makes it difficult for proper scrutiny to occur. It also makes it difficult for the public to be informed of this vast number of changes to the law.

Summary of Topic 2

Parliament gives some of its power to other people and organisations to make laws. It gives this power in an enabling Act.

Types of delegated legislation

1 **Bylaws:** these are made by local councils and other public bodies. Public corporations, such as the buses and train services, are able to impose fines for non-payment of fares.
2 **Statutory instruments:** these are regulations made by government departments to implement the provisions made in Acts of Parliament. For example, the Department of Constitutional Affairs can make changes to the provision of legal aid under the **Legal Aid Act 1998**.
3 **Orders in Council:** these are laws passed by the Privy Council. They have the power to pass laws in times of emergency, with the permission of the Queen, under the **Emergency Powers Act 1920**.

Controls on delegated legislation

1 **General supervision of delegated legislation:** enabling Act, consultation and publication.

2 **Parliamentary supervision of delegated legislation:** bylaws are checked by the relevant government minister; statutory instruments are checked by a select committee of MPs; affirmative resolution procedure; negative resolution procedure; question time.

3 **Court supervision of delegated legislation:** judicial review. An organisation or member of the public may challenge a piece of delegated legislation in the High Court. The judge will interpret the wording of the enabling Act to decide if the law was made *ultra vires* (beyond the powers granted by Parliament) and may declare it void. There are two types of *ultra vires*: substantive *ultra vires*, e.g. *Commissioners of Customs and Excise* v *Cure and Deeley* (1962) and procedural *ultra vires*, e.g. *Agricultural, Horticultural and Forestry Training Board* v *Aylesbury Mushrooms Ltd* (1972). The courts will also declare delegated legislation to be invalid when the law made under the enabling Act is 'unreasonable ('Wednesbury unreasonableness').

Evaluation

1 **Advantages of delegated legislation:** saves time, is flexible and is made by experts.

2 **Disadvantages of delegated legislation:** undemocratic, too much in quantity, scrutiny difficult.

This system tries to create certainty in the law.

The system of judicial precedent involves common law (also known as case law or judge-made law). There are some areas of both criminal and civil law that have not been codified by Parliament. Examples of such laws include the criminal law of murder and the civil law of negligence. The system of precedent ensures that there is a consistent application of these laws in the courts. The doctrine of judicial precedent is based on the Latin term *stare decisis*, which means 'to stand by the decision'.

A Hierarchy of the courts

This is a popular subject for examination questions.

The hierarchy of the courts decides which judges are bound by the precedents of other judges. The superior courts bind the inferior courts and some courts are bound by their own previous decisions.

Precedent is based on judges following the previous decisions of 'higher' courts to try to make the law more certain. This works according to the hierarchy of the courts.

1 House of Lords

The House of Lords is the most senior court in England and Wales. Decisions made here bind all the courts below it. The House of Lords is also bound by its previous decisions. However, it may depart from its previous decision when it appears 'right to do so' (Practice Statement 1966 — see page 21). The House of Lords is bound to follow the decisions of the European Court of Justice if a case involves European Union law.

2 Court of Appeal

The Court of Appeal is bound to follow the decisions of the House of Lords. It is also bound by its own decisions. There are, however, three exceptions to this rule; these were established in the case of *Young* v *Bristol Aeroplane* (1944) (see page 21).

The criminal division of the Court of Appeal has a little more freedom than the civil division because a person's liberty is at stake. The criminal division follows the *Young* v *Bristol Aeroplane* (1944) exceptions but can also refuse to follow a previous case if it thinks the law was misapplied or misunderstood (as occurred in *R* v *Taylor*, 1950).

If the Judicial Committee of the Privy Council decides a case that applies to English law and a majority of the Law Lords have decided to change the law in their capacity as the Judicial Committee of the Privy Council, such a decision can overrule a precedent set by the House of Lords. The Court of Appeal should then follow the Privy Council decision instead of that of the House of Lords. This happened in *Attorney General for Jersey* v *Holley* (2005), where the Privy Council changed the law of provocation. The Court of Appeal in *R* v *James* (2006) was bound to follow the Privy Council decision in Holley instead of the existing House of Lords precedent.

3 *High Court*

The High Court is bound by the courts above it and binds the courts below it.

The divisional High Court (appeal courts in the High Court) is bound by its own past decisions and it binds the High Court ordinary. The Queen's Bench Division has a bit more flexibility (like the criminal Court of Appeal) than the civil Chancery and Family divisions.

The High Court ordinary is not bound by its own past decisions.

4 *Crown Court, County Court and Magistrates' Court*

The inferior courts are not bound by their own decisions, nor do they bind other courts. This is because they do not make precedents; they just apply the precedents set by the higher courts.

B Types of precedent

When a judge/judges decide a case they make a speech explaining what their decision is. This speech is called a judgement.

During the judgement the judge or judges will:
- give a summary of the facts
- give the *ratio decidendi*
- sometimes state *obiter dicta*
- give the verdict

Always define Latin terms and use cases to illustrate.

Ratio decidendi literally means 'the reason for deciding' (the *ratio* is the binding part of the judgement).

Obiter dicta means 'other things said by the way', that is, the judge makes some other comment on the law (i.e. 'If the facts were different, my decision would be…'). An *obiter dictum* is not binding, although other judges may be persuaded by it.

1 *Binding precedent*

A binding precedent is the part of a judgement that other judges have to follow. The *ratio decidendi* (reason for deciding) made by a judge high enough in the hierarchy will bind the future decisions of other judges. When a case involves a point of law, the lawyers for both parties will research past cases in law reports, the internet, journals etc., to find out what decisions have already been made. By doing this, the lawyers can try to speculate the outcome of their own case if the facts are similar to a previous case.

When a higher court makes a decision, that decision is binding on the lower courts and the court in which it was made (with the exception of the House of Lords). A past decision is only binding if the case was heard in an appropriate court in the hierarchy and the facts of the new case are sufficiently similar.

2

Persuasive precedent

A persuasive precedent need not be followed but it may be helpful to a judge making a decision.

If a judge decides to follow a past decision that was not binding, the decision is said to be persuaded.

Persuasive precedents include:

- a decision made in a lower court that is followed in a higher court, e.g. in *R* v *R* (1991) the House of Lords followed the decision of the Court of Appeal when it decided to make marital rape a criminal offence.
- decisions of courts not within the English hierarchy. The Privy Council decision in the Australian case of *Wagon Mound* (1961) has become an important part of the law of negligence. In *Re S* (1992), the Family Division of the High Court was persuaded by US law when it authorised a caesarean section to be performed without the mother's consent.
- the *obiter dicta* (other things said by the way) of another case. In *R* v *Howe* (1987), the House of Lords set the precedent that duress is not a defence for murder. The judges also made an *obiter dictum* that said that duress should not be a defence for attempted murder. In the case of *R* v *Gotts* (1991), the Court of Appeal followed this *obiter dictum*.
- a statement of law made by a dissenting judge.

C Follow, overrule, reverse, distinguish

An easy way to remember the four options is the word 'FORD' which is the first letter of each.

A judge has to decide whether he or she has to follow a precedent that has been already made. The options open to the judge are to: follow (if the case is sufficiently similar to a previous case); overrule (if the case has reached a court that is high enough in the hierarchy and the judge wants to change the law); reverse (alter the verdict of a case heard in a lower court); or distinguish (not follow an existing precedent in a case that has significantly different material facts).

1

Follow

If the facts of a case are significantly similar to an existing precedent, the judge should always follow the previous decision.

2

Overrule

A superior court may overrule the decision of a court below it and therefore change the law. The House of Lords can use the Practice Statement 1966 to overrule one of its earlier decisions (see page 21).

3   Reverse

A superior court may change the outcome of a case from a lower court based on the same law, e.g. the Crown Court applies the existing law and finds the defendant guilty, whereas the Court of Appeal finds the person not guilty when applying the same law.

4   Distinguish

If the facts of a case are significantly different from the facts of an earlier case, the judge does not have to follow the precedent that is already established. An example was in *R* v *Wilson* (1997), where the Court of Appeal distinguished from the decision of the House of Lords in *R* v *Brown and Others* (1993).

5   House of Lords Practice Statement 1966

Before 1966 the House of Lords was bound by its own decisions. This meant that the law was certain but it could not change. In 1966 the House of Lords passed the Practice Statement, which allows it to change one of its previous decisions when 'it appears right to do so'.

An example is *Addie* v *Dumbreck* (1929), which established the law that trespassers who get injured are not able to claim for personal injury from the occupiers of the land. This law was overruled in the case of *British Railway Board* v *Herrington* (1972) by the House of Lords using the Practice Statement 1966.

In criminal law, *R* v *Howe* (1987) overruled *DPP* v *Lynch* (1973) and the law that allowed duress to be used as a defence for murder. The first time the Practice Statement was used in criminal law was in the case of *R* v *Shivpuri* (1986), which overruled *Anderton* v *Ryan* (1985), changing the law regarding attempts to commit impossible crimes.

> Merely citing cases in an exam is not enough. You should also explain the area of law that the case concerned.

6   Court of Appeal: *Young* v *Bristol Aeroplane*

The Court of Appeal should follow its own previous decisions but there are exceptions, which were established in the case of *Young* v *Bristol Aeroplane* (1944). The three exceptions established here are as follows:

- Where there are two previous Court of Appeal decisions that conflict, the Court of Appeal decides which to reject and which to follow.
- Where there is a conflicting House of Lords decision, the Court of Appeal must follow this and reject its past decision.
- Where the previous decision was made *per incuriam* (carelessly or by mistake).

Lord Denning wanted the Court of Appeal to have the same freedoms as the House of Lords. In *Davis* v *Johnson* (1978) the House of Lords reaffirmed the rules set out in the *Young* case — if the Court of Appeal had more flexibility there would be more uncertainty.

Since the **Human Rights Act 1998** the Court of Appeal can go against a previous decision that conflicts with the Act.

> It is important to understand and be able to use cases to explain the Practice Statement and the *Young* v *Bristol Aeroplane* case.

D Law reporting

It is essential that there is an efficient and accurate system of law reporting. Judges have to research decided cases before they make a decision in case a precedent binds them. Nowadays, law reports are available on the internet from providers such as Lexis Nexis.

E Evaluation

1 Should judges make law?

- Parliament is democratically elected, so it would seem that MPs are the best people to make laws for the country.
- Due to lack of parliamentary time, it may be important for some laws to be made by judges.
- Judges are legal experts whereas politicians are not always.
- Judges can change the law much quicker than Parliament and judge-made law avoids the drafting problems associated with statutory interpretation.
- Judges may be biased or out of touch with modern society.
- If the judiciary were more representative of society, it may be more appropriate for it to be involved in law making.

2 Advantages

- The system creates **certainty** within the law.
- The judgements give detailed **practical rules** for other judges to follow.
- The outcome of a new case can be predicted from earlier decisions so that it avoids **unnecessary litigation**.
- **Flexibility** within the system allows the law to develop when necessary and it can be changed quicker than an Act of Parliament can be changed.

'Litigation' means deciding a case in court.

3 Disadvantages

- The **rigidity** of the system of precedent prevents the law being changed.
- **Illogical distinctions** may be made by judges in a case to avoid following a previous decision.
- It is **unpredictable and dependent on chance** that a case will reach a court high enough to be able to change the law.
- The *ratio decidendi* of a case may be difficult to find in the law report and may be misapplied in a future case.
- It is **undemocratic** to allow judges to make laws.

Summary of Topic 3

The system of judicial precedent involves common law (also known as case law or judge-made law). The doctrine of judicial precedent is based on the Latin term *stare decisis*, which means 'to stand by the decision'.

Hierarchy of the courts

The hierarchy of the courts decides which judges are bound by the precedents of other judges. The superior courts bind the inferior courts and some courts are bound by their own previous decisions.

1 The **House of Lords** is the most senior court in England and Wales. Decisions made here bind all the courts below it. The House of Lords is also bound by its previous decisions, unless a change in the law appears 'right to do so' (Practice Statement 1966).

2 The **Court of Appeal** is bound to follow the decisions of the House of Lords. It is also bound by its own decisions. There are, however, three exceptions to this rule, established in the case of *Young* v *Bristol Aeroplane* (1944).

3 The **High Court** is bound by the courts above it and binds the courts below it.

4 The inferior courts (**Crown Court, County Court and Magistrates' Court**) are not bound by their own decisions, nor do they bind other courts.

Types of precedent

1 A **binding precedent** is the part of a judgement that other judges have to follow. The *ratio decidendi* (reason for deciding) made by a judge high enough in the hierarchy will bind the future decisions of other judges.

2 A **persuasive precedent** need not be followed but it may be helpful to a judge making a decision. If a judge decides to follow a past decision that was not binding, the decision is said to be persuaded. Persuasive precedents include a decision of a lower court (e.g. *R* v *R*, 1991), a decision of a court outside the English hierarchy (e.g. *Re S*,1992), an *obiter dicta* (e.g. *R* v *Howe*, 1987), or a statement of law made by a dissenting judge.

Follow, overrule, reverse, distinguish

1 **Follow:** if the facts of a case are significantly similar to an existing precedent, the judge should always follow the previous decision.

2 **Overrule:** a superior court may overrule the decision of a court below it and therefore change the law.

3 **Reverse:** a superior court may change the outcome of a case from a lower court based on the same law.

4 **Distinguish:** if the material facts of a case are significantly different from the facts of an earlier case, the judge does not have to follow the precedent that is already established.

5 **House of Lords Practice Statement 1966:** before 1966 the House of Lords was bound by its own decisions. This meant that the law was certain but it could not change. In 1966 the House of Lords passed the Practice Statement, which allows the Lords to change one of their previous decisions when 'it appears right to do so'. For example, *R* v *Howe* (1987) overruled *DPP* v *Lynch* (1973) and *R* v *Shivpuri* (1986) overruled *Anderton* v *Ryan* (1985).

6 **Court of Appeal: *Young* v *Bristol Aeroplane*:** the Court of Appeal should follow its own previous decisions but there are exceptions, which were established in the case of *Young* v *Bristol Aeroplane* (1944):

a Where there are two previous Court of Appeal decisions that conflict, the Court of Appeal decides which to reject and which to follow.

b Where there is a conflicting House of Lords decision, the Court of Appeal must follow this and reject its past decision.

c Where the previous decision was made *per incuriam*.

Law reporting

It is essential for judges to research decided cases before they make a decision, in case a precedent binds them.

Evaluation

Parliament is democratically elected so it would seem that MPs are the best people to make laws for the country. Due to lack of parliamentary time, it may be important for some laws to be made by judges.

Judges are legal experts whereas politicians are not always.

This topic is a popular examination question for both AQA and OCR.

Statutory interpretation concerns the role of judges when trying to apply an Act of Parliament to an actual case. The wording of the Act may seem to be clear when it is drafted and checked by Parliament, but it may become problematic in the future.

When Parliament wishes to make an Act of Parliament, to change an existing law, to create a whole new law or to codify a common law, correct wording of the statute is essential. Unlike European Union law, UK statutes are given strict definitions to try to create uniformity of decisions by judges across the country. European Union laws tend to outline what the law is meant to achieve and give the judge the flexibility to apply the law in a way that is just. Statutory interpretation is essential to enforce and apply the law.

The English language is not a precise tool and this leads to many problems. Some words have more than one meaning or mean different things when a punctuation mark is added or if read in a different context. The parliamentary draftsmen may have to rush a law through and not think about all the consequences, as in the **Dangerous Dogs Act 1991**, or well-worded statutes may become problematic in the future due to social or technological advances, as in *Royal College of Nursing* v *DHSS* (1981).

This case is described on page 27 in more detail.

A The rules of interpretation

There are two approaches to statutory interpretation, the literal approach and the purposive approach. Judges who use the literal approach base their decision on the words used in the statute, whereas the purposive approach uses more than just the words to find the purpose of the statute. There are also three main rules of statutory interpretation, which judges use to decide a case. These rules are the literal rule, the golden rule and the mischief rule.

1 Literal rule

The judges take the ordinary and natural meaning of the word and apply it, even if it creates an absurd result. Lord Esher said in 1892: 'The court has nothing to do with the question of whether the legislature has committed an absurdity.'

> **R v *Bentham* (2005)**
> Lord Bingham used the literal rule to interpret the **Firearms Act 1968**. Bentham was convicted of having 'in his possession a firearm or imitation firearm'. Bentham had pretended he had a gun during a robbery but it was his fingers in his coat. The House of Lords quashed his conviction, as the word 'possession' would not include a person's own fingers. It confirmed that if the words are clear, the literal rule should be followed.

It is not always enough just to mention the name of a case. Use the facts of the case to illustrate the rules of statutory interpretation.

1.1 Advantages of the literal rule

This rule respects parliamentary sovereignty. Viscount Dilhorne in 1971 said in support of the literal rule: 'If the language is clear and explicit, the court must give effect to it.' He went on to say: 'The words of a statute must not be overruled by the judges, but reform of the law must be left in the hands of Parliament.'

1.2 Disadvantages of the literal rule

Unjust results can be found in the cases of *Whitely* v *Chapell* (1868), *London and North Eastern Railway Co.* v *Berriman* (1946) and, most famously, *Fisher* v *Bell* (1961).

Whitely v *Chapell* (1868)

An Act was passed to make it an offence to commit electoral malpractice (vote more than once). The wording stated that it was an offence to impersonate 'any person entitled to vote'. The defendant impersonated a dead person. As dead people are not entitled to vote, he had not literally committed an offence.

London and North Eastern Railway Co. v *Berriman* (1946)

A railway worker's wife was not allowed to receive compensation for her husband's death at work because he had been doing maintenance on the train track. The Act stated that compensation would only be paid if someone was killed while 'relaying or repairing' the track. This case illustrates the harsh nature of the literal rule.

Fisher v *Bell* (1961)

This case concerned a flick knife displayed in a shop window. Literally, this was not an 'offer for sale', which was specified in the statute. Lord Parker acquitted Bell under the **Restriction of Offensive Weapons Act 1959**, even though it was obvious that this was exactly the sort of behaviour that Parliament intended to stop. Lord Parker justified his decision because the parliamentary draftsmen knew the legal term 'invitation to treat' but failed to include it, so to respect Parliament's sovereignty he had to infer that they had left it out on purpose.

This case and others have led to much criticism of the literal rule. Professor Zander called the literal rule 'irresponsible' and the Law Commission 1969 thought using the literal rule 'assumes unattainable perfection in draftsmanship'. Lord Denning was also a critic of the literal rule, which he said was popular in the nineteenth century but wrong in principle. In a recent case (*Sirius International Insurance* v *FAI General Insurance*, 2004), Lord Steyn argued that the literal rule should be used with caution.

2 *Golden rule*

This rule is an extension of the literal rule. The judge will alter the words in a statute so that it makes sense.

Some examples of the golden rule being put to use include *R* v *Allen* (1872), *Maddox* v *Storer* (1963) and *Adler* v *George* (1964).

R v *Allen* (1872) is an example of the narrow approach of the golden rule.

R v *Allen* (1872)

The wording of the **Offences Against the Person Act 1861** had to be given a different interpretation for the crime of bigamy, because the way it was written meant that the crime could never be committed.

If you cannot remember the name of a case, the facts can still be used as an example of the rule of statutory interpretation.

The broad approach to the golden rule is where the judge understands the meaning of the word but does not apply its literal meaning as it would be undesirable, e.g. in *R* v *Sigworth* (1935).

> **R v Sigworth (1935)**
> The judge did not want a son who murdered his mother to benefit from her will under the **Administration of Estate Act 1925**.

2.1 Advantages of the golden rule

If the literal rule gives an absurd result that was obviously not what Parliament intended, the judge should alter the words in the statute in order to produce a satisfactory result.

2.2 Disadvantages of the golden rule

The golden rule gives too much power to judges and can lead to inconsistency. The Law Commission 1969 said that there is no clear definition of what will constitute an 'absurd result' and what will not.

3 Mischief rule/purposive approach

This rule gives judges the most flexibility when deciding what 'mischief' Parliament intended to stop. This way they can, in fact, ignore the wording of the statute in order to reach the desired outcome.

The mischief rule was established in *Heydon's Case* (1584). When using this rule, a judge should consider what the common law was before the Act was passed, what the problem with that law was, and what the remedy was that Parliament was trying to provide.

Examples of this rule/approach being put to good use include *Smith* v *Hughes* (1960), *Elliott* v *Grey* (1960) and *Royal College of Nursing* v *DHSS* (1981).

> **Smith v Hughes (1960)**
> The defendants were charged with 'soliciting in a street or public place for the purposes of prostitution', contrary to the **Street Offences Act 1959**. They were soliciting from upstairs windows. Lord Parker used the mischief rule to convict as he believed that the 'mischief' that Parliament had intended to stop was people in the street being bothered by prostitutes.

The purposive approach is a much more 'European' style of interpretation. It was used in *Royal College of Nursing* v *DHSS* (1981) to interpret the Abortion Act 1967.

> **Royal College of Nursing v DHSS (1981)**
> The **Abortion Act 1967** was written at a time when only 'registered medical practitioners' (doctors) were authorised to carry out abortions. The case questioned the legality of the involvement of nurses in the modern practice of non-surgical abortions. The purpose of the Act was to stop back-street abortions, not to prevent involvement by nurses.

3.1 Advantages of the mischief rule/purposive approach

Supporters of this approach include Professor Zander, the Law Commission 1969 and Lord Denning. In the case of *Magor and St Mellons* v *Newport Corporation* (1952) Lord Denning said: 'We sit here to find out the intention of Parliament and carry it out, and we do this better by filling in the gaps and making sense of the enactment.' This approach is also more European in style. As the European Union is becoming more important in many areas of UK law, it would be appropriate for the judiciary to start favouring the purposive approach.

3.2 Disadvantages of the mischief rule/purposive approach

This approach does not respect Parliament's sovereignty. Judges may choose to use it in order to reach the decision they want. It has been suggested by Professor Griffith that Lord Denning used the mischief rule in *London Borough of Bromley* v *GLC* (1983) to make sure that the Conservative area of Bromley won its case against the Labour-run Greater London Council for political reasons. Lord Simonds criticised Lord Denning's attraction to 'filling in the gaps'. He thought that any gaps in the law should be amended by Parliament, as it was not the role of judges to do so.

B Other aids to interpretation

1 Intrinsic aids

These are sources within the Act (internal aids). To determine the meaning of a section of an Act of Parliament, the judge may wish to look at other sections in the Act: the definition section, preamble and the long and short titles.

2 Extrinsic aids

These are sources outside the Act (external aids):

- A judge may use a dictionary to look up the definition of a word.
- Legal textbooks may also be a source of guidance when interpreting a statute, e.g. *Smith* and *Hogan Criminal Law*.
- Laws passed since the enactment of the **Human Rights Act 1998** should be compatible with it.
- The judge may look at other similar Acts of Parliament or the common law that went before.
- If the Law Commission or a Royal Commission first published the Act as a report, their findings may aid interpretation.
- The **Interpretation Act 1978** states that masculine includes feminine and singular includes plural.
- When Parliament debates a new law, all that is said during the debate is written down in a book called *Hansard*. Sometimes a judge is faced with a confusing statute and may want to look to see how Parliament intended the law to be applied. It was only in 1993 when the case of *Pepper* v *Hart* first gave

permission for a judge to do this. It was always thought that to ensure the separation of powers, a judge's decision should never be influenced by the government. Now, as a last resort, it may be consulted. The use of *Hansard* is an obvious example of a judge looking for the intentions of Parliament.

- Explanatory notes are included in all Acts passed since 1999.

3 Presumptions

Judges also make presumptions about the wording of a statute. They know that the common law has not been changed unless the Act clearly states it; a criminal offence usually requires a *mens rea* (guilty mind) and the law should not act retro-spectively. Judges presume these things unless the Act specifically states otherwise, e.g. the **European Communities Act 1972** specifically states that some of its sections are to act retrospectively. Examples of a presumption can be found in *Sweet* v *Parsley* (1970) and *R (W)* v *Commissioner of Police of Metropolis and Another* (2005).

> ### *Sweet* v *Parsley* (1970)
> Most criminal offences are fault-based, which means they require the defendant to have committed a guilty act (*actus reus*) and to have a guilty mind (*mens rea*). When the wording of an Act of Parliament does not include a *mens rea* such as intention or recklessness, the judge will presume that Parliament meant to include one. In this case the **Dangerous Drugs Act 1965** stated that it is an offence to be concerned in the management of premises used for drug taking. The defendant rented a house to people who smoked cannabis. She was literally guilty of the offence but Lord Diplock held that even though the Act did not specify a *mens rea*, he presumed that one was necessary for this serious crime. The defendant was found not guilty. The **Misuse of Drugs Act 1971** now contains the *mens rea* 'knowingly'.

> ### *R (W)* v *Commissioner of Police of the Metropolis and Another* (2005)
> This case concerned the **Antisocial Behaviour Act 2003**. The police were not allowed to remove persons under the age of 16 from curfew areas back to their homes, as the Act did not specifically authorise this. The judge commented on the presumption that an Act of Parliament does not give power to the police unless it specifically states it.

4 Latin rules of language

There are also Latin rules of language that aid interpretation: *ejusdem generis*, *expressio unius est exclusio alterius* and *noscitur a sociis*.

4.1 *Ejusdem generis*

The *ejusdem generis* rule states that general words that follow specific ones are to be of the same type as the specific ones, e.g. 'motorbikes, cars and other vehicles'. The other vehicles would probably only include motorised vehicles. The draftsmen would not have meant for skateboards to be included.

> **Powell v Kempton Park Racecourse (1899)**
> In this case the Act specified 'house, office, room or other place used for betting'. As these were all indoor places it was held that the law did not extend to betting taking place outside at the racecourse.

4.2 *Expressio unius est exclusio alterius*

The *expressio unius est exclusio alterius* rule maintains that if the statute specifically states a certain type, other similar things are not to be included, e.g. 'pit bull terrier dogs' does not include any other type of dog.

> **Tempest v Kilner (1846)**
> In this case the Act specified 'goods, wares and merchandise'. The specific nature of the wording meant that 'stocks and shares' were not included.

4.3 *Noscitur a sociis*

The *noscitur a sociis* rule states that a word draws meaning from the other words around it, e.g. where an Act deals with 'motorbikes, cars and fuel', we can assume that it is motor fuel.

> **Beswick v Beswick (1968)**
> In this case the words 'other property' were interpreted by the court to refer to land only. This was because the case concerned the **Law of Property Act 1925**, which related to land law only.

C Suggestions for reform

Both the Law Commission and the Renton Committee have made proposals as to how to improve the rules of statutory interpretation.

1 Law Commission 1967

- More use should be made of intrinsic and extrinsic aids.
- If the wording is ambiguous, the judge should use the purposive approach.

2 Renton Committee 1973

- Acts should be less detailed and Parliament should adopt a more European style of drafting and interpretation (purposive approach).
- Long sentences should be avoided and Acts should contain examples to show how Parliament intended the law to work.

Summary of Topic 4

The rules of interpretation

There are three rules of interpretation:

1 **Literal rule:** this follows the wording of an Act exactly, which means that the judges respect the sovereignty of Parliament. If the wording is ambiguous, however, it can lead to absurdity, e.g. *Fisher* v *Bell* (1961).

2 **Golden rule:** if the literal rule leads to an absurdity, the judge may alter the interpretation of a word or add words until it makes sense. This allows a judge to improve the law without the need for Parliament to redraft the Act, e.g. *R* v *Allen* (1872). However, a judge may use the golden rule and change the intentions of Parliament.

3 **Mischief rule/purposive approach:** the judge ignores the wording of the Act and tries to decide the intentions of Parliament, e.g. *Smith* v *Hughes* (1960). The widest interpretation is the purposive approach, which is more European in style and was utilised in *Royal College of Nursing* v *DHSS* (1981). This rule may give judges too much power to interpret laws made by the democratically elected Parliament, yet it is seen as the best rule by the Law Commission 1967.

Other aids to interpretation

There are intrinsic and extrinsic aids to interpretation.

1 **Intrinsic aids**
   - other sections of the Act, e.g. the long title and definitions section
   - presumptions, e.g. *Sweet* v *Parsley* (1970)
   - Latin rules of language such as *ejusdem generis* (*Beswick* v *Beswick,* 1968), *expressio unius est exclusio alterius* (*Tempest* v *Kilner,* 1846) and *noscitur a sociis* (*Powell* v *Kempton Park Racecourse,* 1899)

2 **Extrinsic aids**
   - dictionary
   - legal textbooks
   - **Human Rights Act 1998**
   - previous common law
   - Law Commission and Royal Commission report findings, which influenced the Act
   - **Interpretation Act 1978**
   - *Hansard* since *Pepper* v *Hart* (1993)
   - explanatory notes

Suggestions for reform

Both the Law Commission 1967 and the Renton Committee 1973 suggested that the judges should adopt the European style of the purposive approach when interpreting Acts of Parliament.

Visit the EU's website:
www.europa.eu

The European Union (EU) was formed by the Treaty of Rome in 1957. Six European countries signed the treaty and agreed to pool their coal and steel production. The purpose of the EU was to prevent future wars and help the countries rebuild their economies after the Second World War. Over the years the EU has grown. It now contains 27 European countries (member states), with three candidate countries currently applying to join — Turkey, Croatia and the former Yugoslav Republic of Macedonia. The EU makes laws relating to a wide range of issues, including the environment and the rights of workers.

A EU institutions

1 Commission

There are 27 commissioners who are 'independent beyond doubt'. They work for the good of the EU rather than for their individual member states. They each have an area of responsibility, e.g. transport or the environment. The Commission has two main roles:

- **Initiator of new laws:** the Commission proposes new laws that the commissioners and their staff consider would be for the benefit of the EU.
- **Guardian of the treaties:** the Commission is responsible for making sure that EU laws are enforced in the member states. If it finds a member state that is in breach of its EU obligations, it will settle the case in the European Court of Justice.

The Commission commenced proceedings against France in 1999 when France refused to lift the British beef ban.

2 European Parliament

There are 785 Members of the European Parliament (MEPs). They are elected every 5 years in their member states and are allocated seats in proportion to the population in their country. The MEPs may join one of the political parties or remain independent, and they elect a president.

The European Parliament is able to reject the Commission's proposed EU budget and it also has power to hold the Commission and Council of Ministers accountable. It produces a report on the Council of Ministers three times a year and has the power to dismiss the whole Commission.

In 1999 the entire Commission resigned after sleaze allegations.

The European Parliament has gradually been given more involvement in the law-making process. It has moved from a position in which it was mainly consulted to having many more areas in which it is asked to cooperate or co-decide. The argument in favour of the European Parliament having more power is that it is democratically elected from the member states and therefore it should have more involvement in the process.

The European Parliament co-decides EU laws concerning education and culture.

3 Council of Ministers

The Council of Ministers decides which of the Commission's proposals should be made into law. There are 27 ministers, one from each member state. The ministers change according to the issue that is being discussed, e.g. for farming matters, the minister for rural affairs will attend.

The Council of Ministers is the 'effective centre of power' when it comes to law making. It has the final say on the majority of proposals from the Commission. It is arguably unfair that some laws can be passed with just a simple majority of support from the ministers or by using the qualified majority voting system, which allows the bigger member states to decide ultimately. However, if all laws required a unanimous vote from the Council of Ministers and approval from the European Parliament, it would make the process of passing any laws extremely long and complicated.

4 European Court of Justice

The European Court of First Instance was formed in 1989 to reduce the workload of the ECJ.

The European Court of Justice (ECJ) is situated in Luxembourg. The 27 judges hold high judicial positions in their home country and are appointed for 6 years. They are assisted by Advocates General (lawyers) who research the cases sent to the court and produce written opinions. These opinions help the member states work out the precedent set by a case, as the ECJ only states the verdict and not its reasoning.

The ECJ has two roles: a judicial role and a supervisory role.

4.1 Judicial role

The ECJ is not bound by its previous decisions.

The judicial role of the ECJ is to decide cases brought against member states or EU institutions. Proceedings against member states can be brought by other member states or by the Commission. The Commission's role as 'guardian of the treaties' allows it to force a member state to abide by EU law.

> **Re Tachographs: EC Commission v UK (1979)**
> The UK was not complying with the strict EU transport laws, which required all heavy goods vehicles to be fitted with a tachograph machine to limit the number of hours a driver is allowed on the road without a break. The European Commission took the UK to the ECJ, which forced the UK to abide by the EU law.

4.2 Supervisory role

The supervisory role is where a case is referred to the ECJ by a court in a member state. If a court in the UK is deciding a case that involves EU law and it is not sure how it should apply, it can refer the case to the ECJ for a decision. An Article 234 referral allows any court or tribunal to refer a question of EU law to the ECJ if it believes 'a decision on that question is necessary to enable it to give a judgement'. Any court can make a referral but they are discouraged due to the expense of doing so. The highest court in the member state usually makes such a referral.

It is important to note that the ECJ is not an appeal court for people who wish to take their case higher than the House of Lords.

> **Marshall v Southampton Area Health Authority (1986)**
> Marshall had been forced to retire from her job. In the UK the retirement age for men was 65 years old yet for women it was 60 years old. Marshall argued that her employer would not have been able to treat a man the same way as they were able to treat her. As this case involved EU laws regarding sex discrimination, the House of Lords referred the case to the ECJ for a decision. The ECJ agreed that Marshall should win her case. The UK subsequently changed the retirement age, making it the same for both men and women.

B How EU laws are made

Each of the institutions has a role in the law-making process. The Commission and Council of Ministers have a fixed role, whereas the European Parliament's role varies depending on the type of law that is being passed.

1 The Commission

The commissioners propose new laws that they and their staff consider would be for the benefit of the EU. They send the draft proposal to the Council of Ministers for approval.

2 Council of Ministers

The Council of Ministers votes on the proposals of the Commission. Some laws require a unanimous vote or a simple majority. Qualified majority voting is where member states may have more votes in relation to the population of their country. This system of voting ensures that decisions get made, as it is sometimes difficult for all the member states to agree.

3 European Parliament

The European Parliament is involved in consultation, cooperation or co-decision.

- **Consultation** is where the European Parliament is asked for its opinion on a draft proposal from the Commission to help the Council of Ministers decide if it wishes to approve it or not. The Council of Ministers does not have to follow the recommendations made by the European Parliament.
- **Cooperation** is used for laws that affect the internal market. The European Parliament is consulted and once the Council of Ministers has approved the proposal, the European Parliament can suggest amendments. The Council of Ministers can ignore these amendments if all of the ministers vote unanimously.
- **Co-decision** is used for laws affecting international agreements. The European Parliament can veto these types of proposals if the Council of Ministers refuses to accept its suggestions for amendments.

C Types of EU laws

The European Union makes laws on a wide range of subjects. It is particularly involved in improving workers' rights and health and safety law so that citizens of the EU can work in different member states and still be governed by the same law. The EU's aim of economic integration between member states means that it makes many laws regarding trade and business. Other areas include transport, agriculture and the environment.

There are three types of EU law: treaties, regulations and directives.

The proposed EU constitution would replace the existing treaties. It has been delayed since the Dutch and French public voted against it.

1 Treaties

Treaties are known as primary legislation. They are the highest form of EU law. They lay down the aims of the communities and create some rights and obligations. Treaties are **directly applicable**, meaning that they automatically become law in the member state without the member state having to do anything. Treaties also have a **direct effect**.

Van Gend en Loos (1963)
The case of *Van Gend en Loos* (1963) stated that citizens in their country's courts could rely upon a clear obligation made by a treaty.

Treaties have vertical and horizontal direct effects.

Treaties have a **horizontal direct effect** (a citizen can rely on the treaty against other individuals such as his or her employer) and a **vertical direct effect** (a citizen can rely on the treaty against his or her government).

Macarthys v *Smith* (1979)
Smith challenged her employer in the courts for paying her male predecessor more wages for the same job. Her case was successful. This case is an example of a treaty having a horizontal direct effect.

2 Regulations

Regulations state specifically what the member state's law should be. They are directly applicable and have a vertical and horizontal direct effect.

Note that regulations also have a vertical and horizontal direct effect.

Leonesio v *Italian Ministry of Agriculture* (1973)
A regulation stated that member states should subsidise dairy farmers who do not produce milk for 5 years (to reduce over-production). Leonesio claimed his money from the Italian government but it refused to pay because it had not passed a law allowing such compensation to be paid. The court held that Leonesio was entitled to his money. The regulation did not require the Italian government to change its laws. The regulation immediately becomes part of the member state's law the moment it is passed by the EU. This is an example of a regulation having a vertical direct effect.

3

Directives

Directives have a vertical direct effect.

Directives are not directly applicable. They require the member state to change its law to produce a certain result but they allow the member state to decide exactly how to do that. The EU imposes a time limit by which the directive must be implemented. A citizen or a member state can rely on a directive in their national courts if the state has failed to meet the time limit or implement the directive properly. This means that directives have a direct effect (established by the European Court of Justice in the case of *Van Duyn* v *Home Office*, 1974).

> **R (*The Mayor and Citizens of Westminster City Council*) v *The Mayor of London* (2002)**
> A citizen can rely on a directive in his or her national courts. This right is for citizens only. A city council was not allowed to rely on a directive in a case of judicial review that challenged the congestion charge in London.

Directives only have a vertical direct effect. This means that the citizen can only rely on a directive against the state. This includes government departments, local councils and organisations such as the NHS.

> **Marshall v *Southampton Area Health Authority* (1986)**
> Marshall was able to rely on a sex discrimination directive against her employers (a state organisation) when she challenged the unequal retirement age for men and women.

The concept of indirect effect was used in the case of *Marleasing* (1990), which allowed the courts of a member state to interpret laws in accordance with a directive.

D The sovereignty debate

When the UK joined the European Union on 1 January 1973 it agreed that EU laws would overrule any existing UK laws that conflicted. The **European Communities Act 1972** made EU laws the supreme form of law but Parliament could repeal this Act of Parliament at any time and take back its power. The EU is only concerned with certain types of law, e.g. trading, business, workers' rights, environment, transport etc. It is not concerned with criminal law, tort or succession. However, in *Commission of the European Communities* v *Council of the European Union* (2005) the European Court of Justice gave the European Commission the power to force the courts of a member state to fine or imprison a person who breaches EU laws. This decision has been widely criticised as it gives the European Commission power in the criminal law of the member states, even though the Commission is unelected.

The UK has lost its sovereignty to the EU for certain areas of law as long as it stays in the European Union. The sovereignty debate concerns the advantages and disadvantages of being in the EU.

Membership of the EU has created a new source of law, a changed role of the courts, and an uncertain future.

1 A new source of law

New laws from the European Union have had a dramatic effect on citizens. There has been a massive improvement of workers' rights with the creation of the minimum wage, a limit on working hours and a multitude of anti-discrimination laws.

> **R v *Secretary of State for Employment ex parte Equal Opportunities Commission* (1994)**
> This case established greater rights for part-time workers due to the fact that most part-time workers are female and therefore it was a type of sexual discrimination.

Membership of the EU has also created more jobs, greater freedom to move, more money and protection for the environment.

2 A changed role for the courts

Acts of Parliament take precedence over judge-made laws. Since the UK joined the EU, judges are to ignore laws made by Parliament if they conflict with EU laws. This happened in the famous case of *R* v *Secretary of State for Transport ex parte Factortame* (1990).

> **R v *Secretary of State for Transport ex parte Factortame* (1990)**
> This case involved a Spanish fishing company that set up a business in the UK. Parliament passed the **Merchant Shipping Act 1988** to prevent the Spanish fishermen from fishing in UK waters. This Act of Parliament was in direct conflict with the Treaty of Rome. The judges in this case applied the EU law rather than the UK law. This case caused a lot of controversy as it demonstrated the power of the EU.

Since the UK joined the EU, the House of Lords is no longer the highest court in England and Wales. It is bound by the decisions of the European Court of Justice (**European Communities Act** s.3(1)).

Judges have also had to adapt their style of interpretation of laws (see Topic 4). EU laws are written less literally than the UK style of drafting. This means that judges have to adopt a more European style when interpreting EU laws (purposive approach). This was a concern raised by Lord Scarman in the case of *Bulmer* v *Bollinger* (1974) (see below). He was anxious that this modern style of drafting laws would cause problems with the traditional ways that judges were used to.

3 An uncertain future

> **Bulmer v *Bollinger* (1974)**
> In this case Lord Denning was concerned that membership of the EU would slowly erode all of the UK's sovereignty. Many euro-sceptics would argue that the EU has gone too far. What started out as a way to improve trading with other countries has become about much more than just coal and steel.

Denning's famous quote stated: 'The Treaty is like an incoming tide. It flows into the estuaries and up the rivers. It cannot be held back.' After the case of *Factortame* (see above), Lord Denning changed his 'incoming tide' to a 'tidal wave'.

Summary of Topic 5

The European Union (EU) was formed by the Treaty of Rome in 1957. It now contains 27 European countries (member states).

EU institutions

1 **Commission:** there are 27 commissioners, each with an area of responsibility. Their two roles are to initiate new laws and to guard the treaties (make sure member states are abiding by the laws).
2 **Parliament:** there are 785 Members of the European Parliament (MEPs). They are elected every 5 years in their member states and are allocated seats in proportion to the population in their country. The European Parliament has gradually been given more involvement in the law-making process. It has moved from a position in which it was mainly consulted to having many more areas in which it is asked to cooperate or co-decide.
3 **Council of Ministers:** this is the 'effective centre of power'. It decides which of the Commission's proposals should be made into law. There are 27 ministers, one from each member state.
4 **European Court of Justice:** this is situated in Luxembourg. The 27 judges hold high judicial positions in their home country and are appointed for 6 years. The ECJ has two roles: its judicial role is to decide cases, e.g. *Re Tachographs: EC Commission* v *UK* (1979) and its supervisory role is to decide cases referred to it from a member state's court (Article 234 referral), e.g. *Marshall* v *Southampton Area Health Authority* (1986).

How EU laws are made

1 The commissioners propose new laws that they and their staff consider would be for the benefit of the EU. They send the draft proposal to the Council of Ministers for approval.
2 The Council of Ministers votes on the proposals of the Commission.
3 The European Parliament is involved in consultation, cooperation or co-decision.

Types of EU laws

1 **Treaties:** these are the highest form of EU law. They lay down the aims of the communities and create some rights and obligations. Treaties are directly applicable and also have a direct effect, e.g. *Van Gend en Loos* (1963) and *Macarthys* v *Smith* (1979).
2 **Regulations:** these state specifically what the member state's law should be. They are directly applicable and have a vertical and horizontal direct effect, e.g. *Leonesio* v *Italian Ministry of Agriculture* (1973).
3 **Directives:** these are not directly applicable. They require the member state to change its law to produce a certain result, yet they allow the member state to

decide exactly how to do that, e.g. *R (The Mayor and Citizens of Westminster City Council)* v *The Mayor of London* (2002) and *Marshall* v *Southampton Area Health Authority* (1986). Directives have only a vertical direct effect.

The sovereignty debate

The UK has lost its sovereignty to the EU for certain areas of law as long as it stays in the European Union. The sovereignty debate concerns the advantages and disadvantages of being in the UK.

1 **A new source of law:** new laws from the European Union have had a dramatic effect on citizens. There has been a massive improvement of workers' rights with the creation of the minimum wage, a limit on working hours and a multitude of anti-discrimination laws, e.g. *R* v *Secretary of State for Employment ex parte Equal Opportunities Commission* (1994).

2 **A changed role for the courts:** Acts of Parliament take precedence over judge-made laws. Since the UK joined the EU, judges are to ignore laws made by Parliament if they conflict with EU laws. This happened in the famous case of *R* v *Secretary of State for Transport ex parte Factortame* (1990).

3 **An uncertain future:** in *Bulmer* v *Bollinger* (1974) Lord Denning was concerned that membership of the EU would slowly erode all of the UK's sovereignty.

The government has control over which laws will be made each year.

The government may be influenced by organisations to change existing laws or to make new ones. It may seek the advice of different organisations to help it formulate its policy. There are official agencies that do research and investigate areas of law that may need updating. Organisations such as the Law Commission and Royal Commissions will suggest proposals for reform of the law to the government. Other influences come from the media, public opinion, pressure groups, Parliament and the judiciary.

A Law Commission

Visit the Law Commission's website: **www.lawcom.gov.uk**

The **Law Commission Act 1965** set up this permanent body. It consists of five legal experts chosen from the judiciary, legal profession and legal academics. Its job is to:

- identify areas of law where reform is necessary
- codify the law
- repeal obsolete laws
- consolidate and modernise the law

The Law Commission is asked to consider specific areas of law referred to it by the Lord Chancellor and may also choose other areas itself to consider. It first researches the law it is considering and then produces a consultation paper to allow experts and politicians to comment. It then produces a final report, which includes a draft bill if it considers that a change to the current law is necessary.

Some Law Commission reports have been successful and include the **Computer Misuse Act 1990**, which created offences related to the hacking of computer systems, and the **Family Law Act 1996**, which changed the law of divorce.

Parliament is not always keen to find time to pass the Law Commission's draft bills. The Draft Criminal Code, for example, rewrote the whole of the criminal law into one document. Such a large piece of legislation would require hours of parliamentary time for it to be properly debated and scrutinised. This is something that the government is, and previous governments have been, reluctant to allow, as it would use up the time that it requires to pass other Acts.

Around 70% of the Law Commission's proposals eventually become law, but a lot of the work that it does is disregarded. The government is not obliged to pass any of the Law Commission's recommendations.

The Law Commission's role of repealing obsolete legislation is more successful.

Statute Law (Repeals) Act 1998
The **Statute Law (Repeals) Act 1998** repealed over 150 complete Acts of Parliament, which were outdated. Such consolidation of the law can pass through Parliament quickly without need for debate.

B Royal Commissions

'Ad hoc' means 'when necessary'.

Royal Commissions are groups of independent experts who are asked to consider a specific area of concern. They are set up on an ad hoc basis and work part time to investigate the issue and then formulate their proposals. After its report is finished, the group disbands. These groups are usually set up when there is a problem with an existing area of law.

The Runciman Commission

The Runciman Commission was set up after the Birmingham Six were released. It was necessary for the government to investigate the criminal justice system to discover why these people were wrongly convicted of the IRA bombing of a pub in Birmingham. The six were imprisoned for 15 years before being finally released. The Commission was led by Viscount Runciman, who investigated police procedure, the court service and the appeal system. He made many recommendations, one of which led to the creation of the **Criminal Appeals Act 1995** and the establishment of the Criminal Case Review Commission, which considers cases where a possible miscarriage of justice has occurred. One of the major proposals of the Runciman Report was to maintain the right to silence. The government, however, ignored this advice and modified it in the **Criminal Justice Act 1994**.

The examiners are particularly keen for you to concentrate on learning the role of the Law Commission and Royal Commissions for this topic.

Other Royal Commission reports include the Pearson Commission 1978 on civil liability, whose recommendations were never implemented. The Philips Commission led to the **Police and Criminal Evidence Act 1984** and the Wakeham Commission looked into the further reform of the House of Lords in 2000.

C Other influences on Parliament

1 Public inquiries

These are usually set up after a serious event or disaster. They are often headed by a senior judge.

Taylor Report

The Taylor Report was set up after the Hillsborough disaster and led to all-seated football stadiums.

Cullen Report

The Cullen Report led to the **Firearms (Amendment) Act 1997**, which banned handguns after the Dunblane disaster.

2

Media

The media may campaign for a change in the law. For example, reports concerning pit bull terriers attacking children led to the **Dangerous Dogs Act 1991**.

Sarah Payne

The *News of the World* newspaper started a campaign after the death of Sarah Payne in 2000. They wanted the government to change the law so that paedophiles would be 'named and shamed'. This media campaign had a lot of backing from the public, yet the government was reluctant to change the existing law. It did, however, lead to a small change in the law.

3

Pressure groups

There is a vast amount of information about pressure groups available on the internet.

The Fathers 4 Justice campaign uses publicity stunts (known as 'direct action'). It has so far been unsuccessful, yet gay rights groups were successful at getting the age of homosexual consent lowered from 18 to 16 in 2000. Pressure groups may 'lobby' Parliament, e.g. trade unions lobby MPs to get better rights for workers. Some pressure groups have 'insider' status, which means that the government consults with them when formulating a new law. The League Against Cruel Sports organisation was influential when the government banned fox-hunting.

The Snowdrop Campaign

This pressure group was set up after the Dunblane massacre, in which 16 children and their teacher were shot at a primary school in Scotland. This small group had the backing of the media and the public. It wanted to ban handguns and it influenced the Cullen Report's recommendation to change the law (see above).

4

Manifesto promises

The government is said to have a 'mandate' (authority) to pass laws promised in a manifesto without too much opposition.

Political parties publish their proposals for new laws in a manifesto in the lead up to a general election. The Labour Party's manifesto in 1997 promised reforms to the House of Lords, which have been done, and the Conservative Party promised the introduction of the poll tax in its 1987 manifesto.

Poll tax

The Conservative Party wrote in its 1987 manifesto that it would introduce a new taxation system called the poll tax. It was to replace the 'rates' system that was used to pay for public services in each council area. The Conservative Party won the election and brought the poll tax into effect. This new tax was not well received by the public and media. There were large protests and demonstrations, with many people preferring to go to prison than to pay it. This pressurised the government to change the poll tax.

5

European Union law

For more on European Union law, visit **www.europa.eu**

If UK law does not conform to EU laws, Parliament must create a new law. For example, the **Sex Discrimination Act 1986** was created to improve protection of female workers.

Summary of Topic 6

The government may be influenced by organisations to change existing laws or to make new ones. It may seek the advice of different organisations to help it formulate its policy.

Law Commission

The **Law Commission Act 1965** set up this permanent body. It consists of five legal experts chosen from the judiciary, legal profession and legal academics. Its job is to identify areas of law where reform is necessary, codify the law, repeal obsolete laws, consolidate and modernise the law, e.g. the **Family Law Act 1996**, which changed the law of divorce.

Parliament is not always keen to find time to pass the Law Commission's draft bills, e.g. the Draft Criminal Code.

The Law Commission's role of repealing obsolete legislation is more successful, e.g. the **Statute Law (Repeals) Act 1998**.

Around 70% of the Law Commission's proposals eventually become law, but a lot of the work that it does is disregarded. The government is not obliged to pass any of the Law Commission's recommendations.

Royal Commissions

These are groups of independent experts that are usually set up when there is a problem with an existing area of law, e.g. the Runciman Commission, the Pearson Commission 1978 and the Wakeham Commission.

Other influences on Parliament

1 **Public inquiries:** these are usually set up after a serious event or disaster, e.g. the Taylor Report (set up after the Hillsborough disaster) and the Cullen Report (set up after the Dunblane massacre).
2 **Media:** the media may campaign for a change in the law, e.g. reports concerning pit bull terriers attacking children led to the **Dangerous Dogs Act 1991**. The campaign to 'name and shame' paedophiles after the murder of Sarah Payne was, however, unsuccessful.
3 **Pressure groups:** the Fathers 4 Justice campaign uses publicity stunts (known as 'direct action'). It has so far been unsuccessful, yet gay rights groups were successful at getting the age of homosexual consent lowered from 18 to 16 in 2000. Pressure groups may 'lobby' Parliament, e.g. trade unions lobby MPs to get better rights for workers. Some pressure groups have 'insider' status, which means that the government consults with them when formulating a new law. The League Against Cruel Sports organisation was influential when the government banned fox-hunting.
4 **Manifesto promises:** political parties publish their proposals for new laws in a manifesto in the lead-up to a general election. The Labour Party's manifesto in 1997 promised reforms to the House of Lords, which have been done, and the Conservative Party promised the introduction of the poll tax in its 1987 manifesto.
5 **European Union law:** if UK law does not conform to EU laws, Parliament must create a new law, e.g. the **Sex Discrimination Act 1986** was created to improve protection of female workers.

It is necessary to know some basics about civil law. It is also important to use the correct legal terminology when explaining the civil courts:

- A civil case is a **dispute** between individuals.
- The **claimant** makes a **claim** against the **defendant**.
- The claimant must find the defendant **liable** on a '**balance of probabilities**'. This is the standard of proof in a civil case.
- The **burden of proof** is on the **claimant** to find the defendant liable.
- If found liable, the defendant must put the claimant back in the position he or she was in before the case.
- The winner of the case will usually be awarded compensation.

A Woolf reforms

1 Problems with the civil courts pre-1999

The Access to Justice report can found at **www.dca.gov.uk**

Lord Woolf issued a report in 1996 called 'Access to Justice'. It outlined the criticisms of the civil court system and suggested proposals for how it could be improved. The County Court and High Court had different procedures, which were complicated and expensive. Cases would suffer delays that would in turn cause more expense to the parties involved. The procedures were too adversarial and did not promote alternative methods of dispute resolution, there was too much emphasis on oral evidence, and the whole process of making a claim was too driven by lawyers.

2 Civil Procedure Rules 1999

The Woolf Report came into force in the Civil Procedure Rules 1999. Its main reforms included:

- greater promotion of alternative dispute resolution
- pre-action protocols that encourage the exchange of documents and evidence before the trial
- judges are to be much more involved in case management, including strict timetabling of cases to reduce delays and setting time limits for how long a trial will run; this allows the parties involved to get a better idea of how much the case is going to cost
- shared Civil Procedure Rules between the County Court and the High Court
- the three-track system (see below)

B The three-track system

A judge will review a case before it goes to court and will allocate it to one of the three tracks: small claims track, fast track or multi-track.

1 Small claims track

Trials are held in the Small Claims Court at the County Court. They are less formal and less adversarial than the normal court procedure. The district judge hears the case with the claimant and defendant and it is not necessary to have a solicitor present. It can hear cases worth up to £5,000 (up to £1,000 for personal injury claims). It is a form of arbitration rather than litigation.

> There is no legal aid available for these cases but they are cheaper and quicker than a formal County Court trial.

2 Fast track

A circuit judge hears these cases in the County Court. They include cases worth between £5,000 and £15,000 (between £1,000 and £50,000 for personal injury). The trial will not last more than 1 day and a trial date is set within 30 weeks.

3 Multi-track

Cases worth more than £15,000 (over £50,000 for personal injury) are allocated to either the High Court or the County Court. The allocation of an appropriate court usually depends on the amount being claimed and/or the complexity of the law involved in the case.

C The civil courts and appeals system

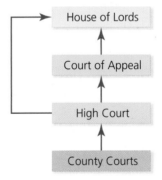

Civil courts routes of appeal

1 House of Lords

The House of Lords is the highest appeal court in England and Wales. Cases concerning European Union law may be referred to the European Court of Justice for a decision (Article 234 referral).

The House of Lords only hears appeals with leave (permission granted by the Court of Appeal or the House of Lords) on a point of law of general public importance.

A leap-frog appeal may be made from the High Court to the House of Lords if the Court of Appeal is already bound by one of its previous decisions.

2 Court of Appeal

The Court of Appeal hears appeals from both the County Court and the High Court regarding any civil matter. It deals with appeals about the facts of the case and points of law raised in the case.

3 High Court

The High Court is a court of first instance for trials involving specific areas of law or claims over £15,000 (£50,000 for personal injury claims). It has three divisions, which each deal with certain types of civil claims. The Queen's Bench Division deals with contract and tort cases as well as judicial review and defamation. It also has a specialist commercial court and an admiralty court. The Family Division deals with divorce and other family matters such as cases involving children and medical treatment. The Chancery Division deals with equity and trusts, taxation, wills and other money-related matters.

The High Court is also an appeal court. The three divisions of the High Court (explained above) are known as the divisional courts when they hear appeals. The Queen's Bench Divisional Court deals with appeals from tribunals, the Chancery can hear an appeal involving land and bankruptcy from the County Court and the Family Divisional Court hears appeals from the Magistrates' Family Court.

4 County Courts

County Courts hear the majority of civil cases. They are local courts and there are approximately 300 around the country. They deal with most divorce cases and cases that are worth less than £15,000 (less than £50,000 for personal injury cases).

The Small Claims Court is part of the County Court. It deals with cases worth less than £5,000. This court uses a less formal procedure (arbitration) to decide liability. The parties in such a case are encouraged to represent themselves and avoid the cost of hiring a solicitor.

5 Magistrates' Court

The Magistrates' Court deals mainly with criminal cases, yet it has some civil jurisdiction over family matters. The Magistrates' Court can approve care orders and adoption orders for children and make provisions for the break-up of a marriage. It cannot, however, grant a divorce.

D Criticisms of the Woolf reforms

The civil court system had many problems, which Lord Woolf tried to address in his 1996 Access to Justice report (see page 44). There are, however, criticisms of the Woolf reforms:

- There has been a dramatic reduction in the number of cases reaching the civil courts. This is due to the pre-action protocols that encourage the use of alternative dispute resolution (ADR — see Topic 8) and out-of-court settlements. Although this seems an advantage of the new system, there are many disadvantages to the people involved in the dispute. Claimants who are not used to the civil court system (known as 'one shooters' by Galanter's study in 1986) may be disadvantaged if they are claiming from 'repeat players' (businesses and insurance companies that are used to using the civil courts). Insurance companies in particular are used to using the civil court system and have specialist lawyers who work for them. This gives an unequal bargaining position to the insurers, who may use the complexity and expense of the courts to force an out-of-court settlement for a much smaller amount.
- Small claims cases seem to be taking longer to resolve since the Woolf reforms.
- The strict procedures and timetabling of cases can hinder the work of the lawyers involved in the case.
- The new early disclosure rules have been seen as a success by the Law Society and the Civil Justice Council in its report, 'More Civil Justice: The Impact of the Woolf Reforms on Pre-action Behaviour' (2002), as it leads to more early settlements.
- In the government's report 'Emerging Findings: An Early Evaluation of the Civil Justice Reforms' (2001) it found that cases are being settled earlier and more people are using ADR.
- The Civil Procedure Rules 1999 have been changed many times with new Practice Directions. This makes it hard for lawyers to keep up with the rules.
- Professor Zander has made many criticisms of the Woolf reforms. He argues that the delays experienced in civil cases are not only due to the adversarial nature of civil justice. These other reasons for delays will mean that civil cases will continue to be lengthy. Statistics published in 2002 by the Court Service indicate that while County Court claims have been tried more quickly (640 days in 1997 compared with 500 days in 2001), High Court cases are on average longer than they were (up to 173 weeks).
- The small claims track is supposed to be less formal. The parties in the claim do not require a lawyer but instead they can represent themselves. There is concern that the claim forms are still too complicated and the court procedures vary as to how informal they actually are. Some small claims cases involve complex areas of law, which it seems unfair for parties of the case to have to contend with without employing a lawyer. This also raises again the inequality of bargaining power. More affluent parties may still employ a lawyer in a small claims case, which will disadvantage the party that has to represent itself.
- If the claimant wins the case and the judge awards damages and makes the defendant pay for the claimant's legal costs, it is difficult to enforce the award, especially if the defendant does not have enough money to pay it.

See the court service website for more statistics: **www.courtservice. gov.uk**

Summary of Topic 7

Woolf reforms

1 **Problems with the civil courts pre-1999:** Lord Woolf issued a report in 1996 called 'Access to Justice'. It outlined the criticisms of the civil court system

(e.g. different and complex court procedures, too expensive and too many delays) and suggested proposals for how it could be improved.

2 **Civil Procedure Rules 1999:** the Woolf Report came into force in the Civil Procedure Rules 1999. Its main reforms included:

- greater promotion of alternative dispute resolution
- pre-action protocols that encourage the exchange of documents and evidence before the trial
- judges are to be much more involved in case management, including strict timetabling of cases to reduce delays and setting time limits for how long a trial will run; this allows the parties involved to get a better idea of how much the case is going to cost
- shared Civil Procedure Rules between the County Court and the High Court
- the three-track system

The three-track system

1 **Small claims track:** trials are held in the small claims court at the County Court. The district judge hears the case with the claimant and defendant and it is not necessary to have a solicitor present. It can hear cases worth up to £5,000 (up to £1,000 for personal injury claims).

2 **Fast track:** a circuit judge hears these cases in the County Court. They include cases worth between £5,000 and £15,000 (between £1,000 and £50,000 for personal injury). The trial will not last more than 1 day and a trial date is set within 30 weeks.

3 **Multi-track:** cases worth more than £15,000 (£50,000 for personal injury) are allocated to either the High Court or the County Court. The allocation of an appropriate court usually depends on the amount being claimed and/or the complexity of the law involved in the case.

The civil courts and appeals system

1 **House of Lords:** this is the highest appeal court in England and Wales. Cases concerning European Union law may be referred to the European Court of Justice for a decision (Article 234 referral). The House of Lords only hears appeals with leave (permission granted by the Court of Appeal or the House of Lords) on a point of law of general public importance. A leap-frog appeal may be made from the High Court to the House of Lords.

2 **Court of Appeal:** this hears appeals from both the County Court and the High Court regarding any civil matter. It deals with appeals about the facts of the case and points of law raised in the case.

3 **High Court:** this is a court of first instance for trials involving specific areas of law or claims over £15,000 (£50,000 for personal injury claims). It has three divisions (the Queen's Bench, Chancery and Family divisions), which each deal with certain types of civil claims. The High Court is also an appeal court. The three divisions of the High Court are known as the divisional courts when they hear appeals. The Queen's Bench Divisional Court deals with appeals from tribunals, the Chancery can hear an appeal involving land and bankruptcy from the County Court and the Family Divisional Court hears appeals from the Magistrates' Family Court.

4 **County Courts:** these hear the majority of civil cases. They are local courts and there are approximately 300 around the country. They deal with most divorce

cases and cases that are worth less than £15,000 (less than £50,000 for personal injury cases).

5 **Magistrates' Court:** this deals mainly with criminal cases, yet it has some civil jurisdiction over family matters. The Magistrates' Court can approve care orders and adoption orders for children and make provisions for the break-up of a marriage. It cannot, however, grant a divorce.

Criticisms of the Woolf reforms

- Small claims take longer, as do High Court cases.
- Too many people may settle out of court.
- The timetabling of cases is too strict.
- The Civil Procedure Rules keep changing.
- The small claims track is still too complicated for the parties to represent themselves.

Alternative dispute resolution (ADR) has become increasingly popular. The civil court system is expensive and time consuming. People are therefore using alternatives to court to solve their disputes. Some types of ADR are as follows:

- **Arbitration** is a less formal procedure than litigation (going to court) but a trained arbitrator makes a binding decision.
- **Mediation** is where an impartial go-between speaks separately to both parties to try to find areas of agreement between the parties. The mediator may suggest a solution to the dispute.
- **Conciliation** is similar to mediation. A conciliator encourages the parties to find an acceptable solution.
- **Negotiation** is where the parties discuss the dispute between themselves in the hope of reaching an agreement.

A Types of ADR

1 Tribunals

A tribunal is composed of three people. One will be legally qualified and the other two will be experienced in the area considered by the tribunal.

Domestic tribunals are used by professional bodies to discipline or resolve disputes within the profession, e.g. the Law Society governs solicitors and has the power to suspend or disbar a member for misconduct.

Administrative tribunals are set up by the government to allow citizens a way to challenge the decisions of powerful organisations. Such tribunals include rent tribunals, social security appeal tribunals, immigration appeals tribunals, mental health tribunals and, most commonly, employment tribunals. They are governed by the **Tribunals and Enquiries Act 1992** and are supervised by the Queen's Bench Division of the High Court.

Tribunals vary in their procedures, with some being similar to a court trial. Not all tribunals have a route for appeal.

2 Arbitration

The parties agree to have their dispute decided by an independent arbitrator. The small claims procedure is a form of arbitration used in the County Court where the judge decides the dispute in a less formal way than in a court case. Many businesses include an arbitration clause (known as a *Scott* v *Avery* clause) in their contracts, which requires both parties to use arbitration should a dispute arise. The organisation ACAS (Arbitration, Conciliation and Advisory Service) uses this method to solve employment disputes and ABTA (the Association of British Travel Agents) uses arbitration to deal with complaints made by holidaymakers.

The **Arbitration Act 1996** states: 'The object of arbitration is to obtain the fair resolution of dispute by an impartial tribunal without unnecessary delay or expense.'

Sir Andrew Leggatt's review of tribunals can be read at
www.tribunals-review.org.uk

3 Mediation

A mediator is an impartial go-between who does not make a decision for the parties but tries to find areas upon which they agree. This form of ADR is only useful if the parties are willing to cooperate. The mediator may meet each party separately. Mediation is used in family disputes and may be appropriate in divorce cases (**Family Law Act 1996**). There are now organisations that provide mediation services, for example the Family Mediators' Association and the UK College of Family Mediators.

4 Conciliation

A conciliator discusses the dispute with the parties and encourages them to find a solution upon which they both agree. Most disputes involving employment try this method before the case goes to an employment tribunal. The organisation ACAS offers this service to encourage an employer and employee to come to an agreement.

5 Negotiation

The parties involved in a dispute discuss the problem between themselves, with or without a lawyer present, to try to find a solution.

B Evaluation

There are advantages and disadvantages of using ADR instead of the civil courts.

1 Advantages

- **Cost.** ADR is either a free service or much cheaper than the formal court procedure. Most types of ADR do not require the parties to pay for expensive legal representation.
- **Speed.** One of the main criticisms of the civil court procedure is the delay experienced when making a claim. ADR is a much quicker way to resolve disputes.
- **Less formal.** The less formal procedures used in ADR mean that it is less intimidating than a court trial.
- **Less adversarial.** ADR is more concerned with reaching an amicable solution between the parties. This differs from the adversarial nature of the civil court, where the emphasis is on winning.

2 Disadvantages

- **Underused.** The Woolf Report hoped that the majority of civil disputes would be resolved through ADR rather than the courts. Many people still have reservations about using ADR and prefer the formal court procedures.

It is necessary to know some basics about criminal law. It is also important to use the correct legal terminology when explaining the criminal courts:

- A crime is an offence that has been committed against the **state**.
- The defendant will be **prosecuted** on behalf of the Crown by the **CPS** (Crown Prosecution Service).
- The prosecution must find the defendant **guilty** '**beyond all reasonable doubt**'. This is the standard of proof in a criminal case.
- The **burden of proof** is on the prosecution to prove the defendant is guilty.
- If found guilty, the defendant will be **sentenced**. This may be a discharge, fine, community-based sentence or a custodial sentence.

A Classifications of crime

There are three types of criminal offence: summary, triable either-way and indictable offences.

1 Summary offences

Assault is a summary offence.

These are the least serious 'petty' crimes. They are triable summarily at the Magistrates' Court.

2 Triable either-way offences

Theft is a triable either-way offence.

These offences may be tried at the Magistrates' Court or at the Crown Court, depending on the circumstances of the case.

3 Indictable offences

Murder is an indictable offence.

These crimes must be tried at the Crown Court. They are the most serious offences.

B Pretrial procedure

1 Bail

When a person charged with a criminal offence attends the Magistrates' Court for the first time, the issue of bail is considered. If the magistrates allow the defendant out on bail it means that he or she can go home until the date of his or her next hearing. If the magistrates think it would be better to keep the defendant in prison until their next hearing, they remand him or her in custody. This is decided by a 'bail application'. The prosecution identifies the type of bail that is appropriate. This is followed by the defence's arguments.

The police are allowed to grant 'street bail' at the time of arrest for the accused to appear at the police station or Magistrates' Court at a later date. They may also

 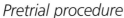

impose conditions to the bail under the **Criminal Justice and Public Order Act 1994**.

1.1 Right to bail

Every defendant has the right to bail, with the exception of a defendant who commits an either-way or indictable offence while on bail. These rules are governed by s.4 **Bail Act 1976**.

It is rare for bail to be granted in murder, manslaughter and rape cases, according to s.54 **Crime and Disorder Act 1988**.

1.2 Exceptions to the right to bail

A defendant will not be granted bail if the court has **substantial grounds** to believe one or more of the following:

- The defendant will fail to surrender to bail (will not turn up for his or her next hearing).
- The defendant is already on bail for another indictable offence.
- The defendant will interfere with witnesses.
- The defendant has broken his or her bail conditions in the past.
- The defendant needs to be remanded in custody for his or her own protection.
- The court has not had enough time to find out if it should grant bail.
- The defendant would commit more crimes if he or she were granted bail.

1.3 Withholding bail

If the court believes that one of the exceptions to the right to bail applies to the defendant, there must be substantial grounds for holding this belief and the court must specify why the defendant is not granted bail.

1.4 Appeals

If the defendant was not granted bail (he or she is being held in custody until the trial) they can appeal at their next court hearing (8 days later) or apply to a Crown Court judge for bail.

The prosecution is allowed to appeal at the next hearing when it believes the defendant should not have been granted bail under the **Bail Amendment Act 1993**.

1.5 Penalty

The penalty for failure to surrender to bail can be a fine of up to £5,000 or imprisonment for up to 12 months.

1.6 Types of bail

Bail can be conditional or unconditional. Bail conditions could include: reporting to the police station every day, living at a certain address, surrendering one's passport, providing surety, being under a curfew, or not being permitted to contact others involved in the case, e.g. witnesses or the victim. These conditions are contained in s.3 **Bail Act 1976**.

Approximately 50,000 offences are committed each year by someone who is on bail.

The magistrates also take into account the seriousness of the crime, the defendant's character and whether he or she has committed any crimes while on bail in the past.

Withholding bail is used to protect the public but it must not be overused. Remanding a person in custody may be in breach of the **Human Rights Act 1998**.

One in 15 people remanded in custody are acquitted at their trial. There is no compensation available to these people.

2 *Mode of trial*

A mode of trial hearing decides whether an either-way offence should be tried at the Magistrates' Court or whether it should be committed to Crown Court.

2.1 Plea

Section 17A **Magistrates' Courts Act 1980** requires the Magistrates' Court to read out the charge to the defendant and ask him or her to indicate whether he or she would plead guilty or not guilty if the case were to go to trial.

2.2 Guilty plea

'Jurisdiction' means the power of the court. The Magistrates' Court has the power to sentence up to 12 months' imprisonment or a £5,000 fine.

If the defendant pleads guilty and the Magistrates' Court accepts jurisdiction, it will convict the defendant and sentence him or her under s.17A **Magistrates' Courts Act 1980**. If the magistrates wish the defendant to receive a sentence that is longer than they have the power to make, they will commit the case to the Crown Court for a sentence under s.3 **Powers of Criminal Courts (Sentencing) Act 2000**.

2.3 Not guilty plea

If the defendant pleads not guilty and the magistrates believe a summary trial is more suitable, they will explain this to the defendant (s.20 **Magistrates' Courts Act 1980**). If the defendant consents to a summary trial, a date will be set. If the defendant does not wish to have the case tried summarily, the case will be sent to Crown Court under s.51 **Crime and Disorder Act 1988**. The defendant is allowed to ask the magistrates to indicate whether they would consider a non-custodial sentence if the defendant were to have a summary trial and plead guilty. The magistrates do not have to give an indication but if they do indicate a non-custodial sentence, they must stick to that decision under s.20A **Magistrates' Courts Act 1980**.

The defendant may opt for a jury trial as juries have a lower conviction rate than magistrates.

If the magistrates decide that the case would be better tried on indictment at the Crown Court they will inform the defendant and commit him or her under s.51 **Crime and Disorder Act 1988**.

3 *Committal*

If the defendant is to have his or her case heard at the Crown Court, the magistrates must first commit the case. This procedure is known as a committal. Indictable offences do not need to be committed to Crown Court. They will be sent directly under s.51 **Crime and Disorder Act 1998**.

If the case is triable either way, the Magistrates' Court will hold committal proceedings, which include a summary of the facts and law by the prosecution. This is a paper-based hearing (no witnesses need to attend) and is governed by rule 7 of the Magistrates' Courts Rules 1981. At the end of the hearing the magistrates will decide if there is sufficient evidence to commit the case to Crown Court. This test is set out in s.6(1) **Magistrates' Courts Act 1980**.

C The criminal courts and appeals system

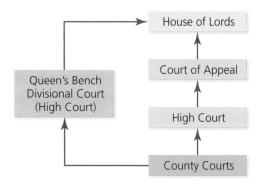

Criminal courts routes of appeal

1 Magistrates' Court

All criminal cases start at the Magistrates' Court. They deal with preliminary matters such as bail applications and legal aid. They have the power to try all summary offences and may try either-way offences if the defendant chooses to have the case heard at the Magistrates' Court. The magistrates have the power to sentence a defendant to up to 12 months in prison. They can also fine the defendant up to £5,000. If the magistrates accept jurisdiction in an either-way offence, and then wish to sentence the defendant to longer than 12 months in prison, they will send the case to the Crown Court for the sentence.

Indictable offences are sent to the Crown Court for trial.

The Magistrates' Court also has specially trained magistrates who deal with young offenders in the Youth Court.

2 Crown Court

The Crown Court tries indictable offences and either-way offences if the defendant has requested that his or her trial be held at the Crown Court. If the defendant pleads guilty, the judge alone will impose a sentence. If the defendant pleads not guilty, a jury will try the case and if found guilty, the judge will impose a sentence.

A case decided in the Magistrates' Court may be appealed to the Crown Court, where a circuit judge and two magistrates will retry a case in which the defendant believes that he or she was wrongly convicted (based on the facts of the case) or that the sentence is too harsh. The Crown Court does not hear appeals concerning a point of law. These are appealed from the Magistrates' Court to the Queen's Bench Divisional Court at the High Court.

3 Court of Appeal

Permission to appeal is known as 'with leave' and is granted by the Crown Court or the Court of Appeal.

The prosecution may appeal to the criminal division of the Court of Appeal if it believes a defendant has received too lenient a sentence or if it believes a defendant was wrongly acquitted, so that the law is changed for the future.

The defence may appeal if it believes the sentence was too harsh (without permission), or against conviction either on a point of law or fact (with permission). An appeal regarding the facts of the case requires new evidence before an appeal is allowed. The Criminal Case Review Commission may recommend that the Court of Appeal allow an appeal in a case where it believes a miscarriage of justice has occurred.

The Court of Appeal can dismiss the appeal, vary a sentence, order a retrial or quash the conviction.

4 *House of Lords*

The House of Lords is the highest appeal court in England and Wales. The House of Lords only hears appeals with leave (permission granted by the Court of Appeal or the House of Lords itself) on a point of law of general public importance.

Cases concerning human rights issues may be appealed further to the European Court of Human Rights. The House of Lords may refer a case concerning European Union law to the European Court of Justice for a decision. This is known as an Article 234 referral.

Summary of Topic 9

Classifications of crime

There are three types of criminal offence:

1 **Summary offences:** these are the least serious, 'petty' crimes. They are triable summarily at the Magistrates' Court, e.g. assault.
2 **Triable either-way offences:** these offences may be tried at the Magistrates' Court or at the Crown Court, depending on the circumstances of the case, e.g. theft.
3 **Indictable offences:** these crimes must be tried at the Crown Court. They are the most serious offences, e.g. murder.

Pretrial procedure

1 **Bail**
   - When a person charged with a criminal offence attends the Magistrates' Court for the first time, the issue of bail is considered. If the magistrates allow the defendant out on bail it means that he or she can go home until the date of his or her next hearing. If the magistrates think it would be better to keep the defendant in prison until the next hearing, they will remand the defendant in custody.
   - Every defendant has the right to bail, with the exception of a defendant who commits an either-way or indictable offence while on bail. These rules are governed by s.4 **Bail Act 1976**.
   - A defendant will not be granted bail if the court has **substantial grounds** to believe one or more of the following: the defendant will fail to surrender to bail (will not turn up for the next hearing), the defendant is already on bail for another indictable offence, the defendant will interfere with witnesses etc.

- Bail can be conditional or unconditional. These conditions are contained in s.3 **Bail Act 1976**.

2 **Mode of trial:** a mode of trial hearing decides whether an either-way offence should be tried at the Magistrates' Court or should be committed to Crown Court.

3 **Committal:** if the defendant is to have his or her case heard at the Crown Court, the magistrates must first commit the case.

Criminal courts

1 **Magistrates' Court:** this has the power to try all summary offences and may try either-way offences if the defendant chooses to have the case heard at the Magistrates' Court. The magistrates have the power to sentence a defendant to up to 12 months in prison.

2 **Crown Court:** this tries indictable offences and either-way offences if the defendant has requested that his or her trial be held at the Crown Court. If the defendant pleads guilty, the judge alone will impose a sentence. If the defendant pleads not guilty, a jury will try the case and if found guilty, the judge will impose a sentence.

3 **Court of Appeal:** the prosecution may appeal to the criminal division of the Court of Appeal if it believes a defendant has received a lenient sentence or if it believes a defendant was wrongly acquitted, so that the law is changed for the future. The defence may appeal if it believes the sentence was too harsh (without permission), or against conviction either on a point of law or fact (with permission). An appeal regarding the facts of the case requires new evidence before an appeal is allowed.

4 **House of Lords:** this is the highest appeal court in England and Wales. The House of Lords only hears appeals with leave (permission granted by the Court of Appeal or the House of Lords itself) on a point of law of general public importance.

The power of the police to stop and search individuals is fundamental to their ability to do their job — namely to prevent and detect crime. The use of this power also necessitates intrusion into the rights of individuals to conduct their lives without interruption. Parliament has tried to ensure that a balance is struck between allowing the police to carry out their role effectively and protecting the rights of individuals.

A Stop and search

The main police powers to stop and search are contained in the **Police and Criminal Evidence Act 1984** (PACE), although other statutes also contain stop and search powers. These include the **Misuse of Drugs Act 1971**, the **Criminal Justice and Public Order Act 1994** and the **Terrorism Act 2000**.

To supplement the statute, the Home Office has issued codes of practice which detail the provisions in PACE. These codes of practice are updated as police powers change. They are not part of the statute itself but breach of these codes may lead to any evidence that has been obtained being ruled inadmissible during any subsequent trial.

> Read the question carefully: it will be asking for information about police powers either in the street or at the station and you must make sure that your answer deals with the correct area.

1 Powers to stop and question

> For higher marks, add cases to illustrate your answers.

The police may question individuals, but those individuals are entirely free to decline to answer unless arrested. This was confirmed in the case of *Rice* v *Connolly* (1966).

> **Rice v Connolly (1966)**
> A member of the public was considered to be behaving suspiciously in an area where several burglaries had occurred. The police questioned the individual but he refused to answer. His conviction for obstructing a police officer in the execution of his duty was quashed and it was confirmed that members of the public are not under any obligation to answer questions.

There is a thin line between lawfully refusing to answer questions and obstructing the police.

> **Ricketts v Cox (1982)**
> The police asked an individual questions about an assault. He was hostile and used abusive language. Magistrates decided that he was guilty of obstruction.

2 The recording of stops

> A record need not be made if the police are asking for general information, looking for witnesses or giving directions.

When an officer requests a person in a public place to account for his or her presence, behaviour or possession of anything, a record must be made of this and a copy given to the person questioned. The record must include the date, time, place, reason why the person was questioned, the individual's definition of his or her ethnicity and the outcome.

3 *Search*

The power to search an individual also comes under s.1 of PACE and is supplemented by Code A. A search occurs when the police stop an individual and search him or her, his or her clothes or anything that he or she is carrying. Code A states that powers to stop and search must be used fairly, with respect and without discrimination. An individual can only be stopped and searched if the police have reasonable suspicion that the suspect has drugs, weapons or stolen property, or things that could be used to commit a crime, an act of terrorism or criminal damage. The suspicion should be based on facts, intelligence, information or behaviour. It cannot be based on personal factors, including age, race, religion, appearance, previous convictions or generalisations, stereotypes or any of these factors in combination.

An individual must be informed that he or she is being stopped so that a search may be carried out. He or she must be informed of the officer's name or number and the station to which the officer is attached, given an explanation of the grounds upon which the search is being carried out and informed of the object of the search. If the officer is not in uniform, he or she must provide identification (PACE s.2(3)).

An individual can be stopped and searched in a public place or anywhere else if the police believe that the person has committed a crime. If the search is in a public place, the suspect can only be required to remove his or her coat or jacket and gloves. If the police wish the suspect to remove anything else, they must take him or her to a nearby place out of public view. If the individual protests, reasonable force may be used (PACE s.117). If the police recover any stolen or prohibited articles, these can be seized (PACE s.1(6)).

The police must provide a written record following the search, which must be done at the time, unless there are exceptional circumstances. This differs slightly from the record made for stops (see above). The record should include the name or a description of the individual, his or her self-defined ethnic background, the date, time and place, a reason for the search and the outcome of it, including any injury or damage sustained.

B Powers of arrest

The powers of arrest under PACE have been amended by the **Serious Organised Crime and Police Act 2005** and a new code. Code G has been issued giving guidance on the exercise of the powers of arrest.

Code G confirms that the right to liberty is a fundamental human right and since the power of arrest interferes with that right, officers must be fully justified in using it. It states that two tests must be met before an arrest can be said to be lawful:

  a The person must be involved or suspected of involvement or attempted involvement in a crime.

  b There must also be reasonable grounds for believing that the arrest is necessary.

An accurate description of this procedure will enhance an answer on police powers of arrest.

1 Procedure

The person must be informed by the arresting officers of the fact of his or her arrest and the reason for it — even if this is obvious. He or she must be cautioned in the following way: 'You do not have to say anything. But it may harm your defence if you do not mention when questioned something which you later rely on in court. Anything you do say may be given in evidence.'

2 Who can be arrested?

The police are permitted to arrest:
- anyone who is about to commit an offence or who is committing an offence
- anyone the officer has reasonable grounds for suspecting is about to commit an offence
- anyone who is reasonably suspected of being guilty of an offence that the officer has reasonable grounds for suspecting has been committed, or anyone guilty of an offence that has been committed

3 The necessity test

The powers of arrest, which apply to any offence, are subject to the necessity test — the officer must believe that it is necessary to arrest that person. Reasons why an arrest might be necessary are set out in s.2 of Code G and include the need to:
- ascertain the name of the person involved or his or her address
- prevent the person causing injury to him- or herself or others
- prevent the person causing damage to property

4 Record of arrest

At the time of arrest or as soon as possible afterwards, the arresting officer is required to record the nature and circumstances of the offence leading to the arrest, the reason why arrest was considered necessary, the fact that a caution was given and anything said by the person at the time of arrest. This information will then be recorded in the custody record on arrival at the station.

C Detention

1 Arrival at the station

Once arrested, the suspect must be taken to the police station as soon as possible. On arrival at the station, he or she will be taken to the custody officer who will assess the strength of the evidence against the person. On the basis of this, the custody officer will decide whether the suspect can be charged. If so, the suspect will be charged and usually released on bail.

If there is not enough evidence to charge the suspect at that stage, he or she will be detained so that the police have time to gather the necessary evidence. Often,

police will try to obtain the required evidence by interviewing the suspect. The suspect has a right to have someone informed of his or her detention and to be told where he or she is being held. This can be delayed if the detention relates to an indictable offence and the delay is considered necessary to protect evidence or prevent harm to others.

2 Time limits

The police are not allowed to detain a suspect indefinitely and the custody officer is required to review the need for detention on a regular basis. The custody officer will review whether there is enough evidence to charge after the first 6 hours. Further reviews will be carried out every 9 hours. Generally, the police can detain suspects for up to 36 hours, timed from their arrival at the station. This may be extended for a further 12 hours by the police themselves but it must be done by an officer of superintendent rank or above. A further and final extension of up to 96 hours is permitted, but this must be approved by a magistrate.

> You will need to learn the relevant time limits for the exam.

3 Interview

Police usually detain suspects so that they can question them about the offence. Often, the police will be aiming to get the suspect to confess, which means that they can bring their investigations to an end relatively quickly and cheaply. Since this might be used as a tool of oppression by the police, safeguards are in place as the interview must be taped and a record made of it afterwards. Additionally, the suspect has the right to consult a legal advisor, but this may be delayed for up to 36 hours.

D Search at the station

On arrival at the station, the suspect is searched and the custody officer records any property. The police can remove anything that they reasonably believe the individual may use to cause physical injury to him- or herself or others, to damage property, interfere with evidence, assist the suspect to escape or is reasonably believed to be evidence (PACE s.54).

1 Non-intimate searches

Fingerprints and other non-intimate samples may then be taken. These can be taken without consent and include oral swabs, saliva, footwear impressions and photographs.

2 Strip search

A strip search or search of the mouth may be carried out if necessary to remove an article that a person would not be allowed to keep. This must be done by an officer of the same sex.

3 *Intimate searches*

Under s.55 of PACE, if a superintendent or superior officer has reasonable grounds for believing that the suspect may have concealed anything which he or she could use to injure him- or herself or others or may have concealed drugs, then he or she can authorise a qualified doctor or nurse to carry out a search of the suspect's bodily orifices.

4 *Intimate samples*

Under s.62 of PACE, intimate samples, some of which require the suspect's consent, can be taken. These include blood, urine, semen, dental impressions, pubic hair and tissue.

E Safeguards

Safeguards are about protecting the rights of the individual and are usually asked about in the evaluation question of an exam.

Parliament has tried to ensure that safeguards are in place so that a balance can be struck between individual rights and the ability of the police to carry out their role effectively.

1 *Stop and search*

Under Code A, a record must be made when an officer requests a person in a public place to account for his or her presence, behaviour or possession of anything and a copy given to the person questioned. The record must include the date, time, place, reason why the person was questioned, the individual's definition of his or her ethnicity and the outcome.

PACE s.1(3) states that a constable only has the power to search if he or she has reasonable grounds for suspicion. Code A states that the power must be used fairly, and without discrimination. Code A also sets out the grounds on which reasonable suspicion can be based. Personal factors cannot be used to justify a suspicion. According to s.2(9), the search must be carried out in public and the person can only be asked to remove his or her coat or jacket and gloves. Code A requires that the suspect be taken to a nearby place out of public view if the police require the removal of any other items of clothing.

The police must have a reason for carrying out a search — Code A states that police cannot stop a person in order to find grounds for a search (sometimes referred to as a 'fishing expedition').

Before being searched, a suspect must be informed of the officer's name or number and the station to which the officer is attached, given an explanation of the grounds upon which the search is being carried out and informed of the object of the search. If the officer is not in uniform, he or she must provide identification. Only reasonable force may be used (PACE s.117).

Under s.3, the police must provide a written record following the search, which must be done at the time, unless there are exceptional circumstances. It should

include the name or a description of the individual, his or her self-defined ethnic background, the date, time and place, a reason for the search and the outcome of it, including any injury or damage sustained.

2 Arrest

The police can only arrest those who are involved or suspected of involvement in a crime and only if they have reasonable grounds for believing that an arrest is necessary. Reasons why an arrest might be necessary are given in Code G. On arrest, the suspect must be told that he or she is under arrest and why (s.28). He or she must then be cautioned (Code C) and under s.30 taken to a police station as soon as practicable. Only reasonable force may be used (s.117).

A record should be made at the time of arrest or as soon as possible afterwards, noting the nature and circumstances of the offence leading to the arrest, the reason why arrest was considered necessary, the fact that a caution was given and anything said by the person at the time of arrest. This information will then be recorded in the custody record on arrival at the station (Code C).

3 At the station

Suspects should be informed that they are allowed to consult the Codes of Practice.

According to s.56 and Code C, any person arrested and held in custody can have someone told of his or her whereabouts. This can be delayed for up to 36 hours if the person is detained in connection with an indictable offence and an officer of superintendent rank or above believes it will lead to interference with evidence, interference or harm to other people, 'tipping off' of others or hinder the recovery of property.

S.58 allows a suspect to consult privately with a solicitor free of charge. This right may be suspended for up to 36 hours for the same reasons as under s.56.

4 Search after arrest

Under s.54, the custody officer makes a record of the suspect's property on arrival at the station. The police can only remove items that they reasonably believe the individual may use to cause physical injury to him- or herself or others, to damage property, to interfere with evidence, to assist the suspect to escape or that are reasonably believed to be evidence (PACE s.54).

Fingerprints and other non-intimate samples can be taken without consent and include oral swabs, saliva, footwear impressions and photographs.

A strip search or search of the mouth may be carried out if necessary, but only if there are reasonable grounds for suspecting that it is necessary to remove an article that a person would not be allowed to keep. This must be done by an officer of the same sex.

Under s.55 of PACE, there must be reasonable grounds for believing that the suspect may have concealed something that he or she could use to injure him- or herself or others with or may have concealed drugs. This requires the authority of

a superintendent or a superior officer, and can only be carried out by a qualified doctor or nurse.

Under s.62 of PACE, intimate samples may require the suspect's consent.

5 Detention

The custody officer is required to review the need for detention on a regular basis. The first review is carried out after 6 hours. Further reviews are carried out every 9 hours. Generally, the police can detain suspects for up to 36 hours, timed from their arrival at the station. This may be extended for a further 12 hours by an officer of superintendent rank or above. A further and final extension of up to 96 hours is permitted, but this must be approved by a magistrate.

> Don't forget to mention the role of the custody officer in your answer.

6 Interview

Section 60 of PACE requires that interviews are recorded. Occasionally, the police may try to circumvent this safeguard by asking the suspect questions somewhere else beforehand — for example in the police car on the way to the station. Once completed, the police must make a separate record of the interview.

7 Treatment of suspects

Under Code C, a suspect is entitled to breaks for meals, refreshments and sleep. Interview rooms must be adequately lit, heated and ventilated, and the suspect should be able to sit down.

8 Additional safeguards

Under s.57, if the suspect is under the age of 17, an appropriate adult must be told that the suspect is being detained and given the reasons why and the location. The appropriate adult should be asked to attend the police station and can be present during any interviews. Under Code C, this also applies to those with mental disorders or handicap.

Summary of Topic 10

The power of the police to stop and search individuals is fundamental to their ability to do their job — namely to prevent and detect crime.

Stop and search

The main police powers to stop and search are contained in the **Police and Criminal Evidence Act 1984**.

1 **Powers to stop and question:** the police may question individuals but those individuals are entirely free to decline to answer unless arrested. This was confirmed in the case of *Rice* v *Connolly* (1966). There is a thin line between lawfully refusing to answer questions and obstructing the police (see *Ricketts* v *Cox*, 1982).

2 **The recording of stops:** when an officer requests a person in a public place to account for his or her presence, behaviour or possession of anything, a record must be made of this and a copy given to the person questioned.

3 **Search:** the power to search an individual also comes under s.1 of PACE and is supplemented by Code A.

Powers of arrest

The powers of arrest under PACE have been amended by the **Serious Organised Crime and Police Act 2005** and Code G has been issued giving guidance on the exercise of the powers of arrest.

1 **Procedure:** the person must be informed by the arresting officers of the fact of his or her arrest and the reason for it — even if this is obvious. He or she must be cautioned in the following way: 'You do not have to say anything. But it may harm your defence if you do not mention when questioned something which you later rely on in court. Anything you do say may' be given in evidence.'

2 **Who can be arrested?:** the police can arrest:

- anyone who is about to commit an offence or who is committing an offence
- anyone the officer has reasonable grounds for suspecting is about to commit an offence
- anyone who is reasonably suspected of being guilty of an offence that the officer has reasonable grounds for suspecting has been committed or anyone guilty of an offence that has been committed

3 **The necessity test:** the powers of arrest, which apply to any offence, are subject to the necessity test — the officer must believe that it is necessary to arrest that person.

4 **Record of arrest:** at the time of arrest or as soon as possible afterwards, the arresting officer is required to record the nature and circumstances of the offence leading to the arrest, the reason why arrest was considered necessary, the fact that a caution was given and anything said by the person at the time of arrest.

Detention

1 **Arrival at the station:** once arrested, the suspect must be taken to the police station as soon as possible.

2 **Time limits:** the police are not allowed to detain a suspect indefinitely and the custody officer is required to review the need for detention on a regular basis. The custody officer reviews whether there is enough evidence to charge after the first 6 hours. Further reviews are carried out every 9 hours. Generally, the police can detain suspects for up to 36 hours, timed from their arrival at the station. This may be extended for a further 12 hours by the police themselves but it must be done by an officer of superintendent rank or above. A further and final extension of up to 96 hours is permitted, but this must be approved by a magistrate.

3 **Interview:** police usually detain suspects so that they can question them about the offence.

Search at the station

On arrival at the station, the suspect is searched and the custody officer records any property. The police can remove anything that they reasonably believe the individual may use to cause physical injury to him- or herself or others, to damage property, to interfere with evidence, to assist the suspect to escape or is reasonably believed to be evidence under PACE s.54.

1 **Non-intimate searches:** fingerprints and other non-intimate samples may then be taken. These can be taken without consent and include oral swabs, saliva, footwear impressions and photographs.

2 **Strip search:** a strip search or search of the mouth may be carried out if necessary to remove an article that a person would not be allowed to keep. This must be done by an officer of the same sex.

3 **Intimate searches:** under s.55 of PACE, if a superintendent or superior officer has reasonable grounds for believing that the suspect may have concealed anything which he or she could use to injure him- or herself or others or may have concealed drugs, then the officer can authorise a qualified doctor or nurse to carry out a search of the suspect's bodily orifices.

4 **Intimate samples:** under s.62 of PACE, intimate samples, some of which require the suspect's consent, can be taken. These include blood, urine, semen, dental impressions, pubic hair and tissue.

Safeguards

1 **Stop and search:** under Code A, a record must be made when an officer requests a person in a public place to account for his or her presence, behaviour or possession of anything and a copy given to the person questioned. Code A states that the power must be used fairly, and without discrimination. Code A also sets out the grounds on which reasonable suspicion can be based. Code A requires that the suspect be taken to a nearby place out of public view if the police require the removal of any items of clothing other than the suspect's coat or jacket and gloves. Code A states that police cannot stop a person in order to find grounds for a search — sometimes referred to as a 'fishing expedition.' Only reasonable force may be used (PACE s.117).

2 **Arrest:** reasons why an arrest might be necessary are given in Code G. On arrest, the suspect must be told that he or she is under arrest and why (s.28). The suspect must then be cautioned (Code C) and under s.30 taken to a police station as soon as practicable. Only reasonable force may be used (s.117).

3 **At the station:** suspects should be informed that they are allowed to consult the Codes of Practice. Under s.56 and Code C, any person arrested and held in custody can have someone told of his or her whereabouts. This can be delayed for up to 36 hours. Section 58 allows a suspect to consult privately with a solicitor free of charge. This right may be suspended for up to 36 hours for the same reasons under s.56.

4 **Search after arrest:** fingerprints and other non-intimate samples can be taken without consent and include oral swabs, saliva, footwear impressions and photographs. Under s.55 of PACE, there must be reasonable grounds for believing that the suspect may have concealed anything that he or she could use to injure him- or herself or others or may have concealed drugs. Under s.62 of PACE, intimate samples may require the suspect's consent.

5 **Detention:** the custody officer is required to review the need for detention on a regular basis.

6 **Interview:** s.60 of PACE requires that interviews are recorded.

7 **Treatment of suspects:** under Code C, a suspect is entitled to breaks for meals, refreshments and sleep.

8 **Additional safeguards:** under s.57, if the suspect is under the age of 17, an appropriate adult must be told that he or she is being detained and given the reasons why and the location.

If someone pleads guilty or is found guilty after a trial then the magistrates or judge, depending upon the type of court, must decide what will happen to the person. The courts have a range of options open to them, including sending an offender to prison or requiring him or her to pay a fine. The option that is chosen will be based on many factors, including the type of offence, the minimum/maximum sentence available, the circumstances of the offence, the age of the defendant, his or her background and the aims of sentencing. Often, the court will order a pre-sentencing report to be compiled by the probation service, which looks at the offender and the crime in greater detail.

A Aims of sentencing

When deciding upon an appropriate sentence to impose, the courts will have regard to at least one of the aims of sentencing. Usually all sentences will include an element of retribution, but the court may want to reduce the chances of the offender committing further offences or might require him or her to make amends for the crime. Section 142 of the **Criminal Justice Act 2003** sets out five main aims of sentencing adult offenders.

You will need to be able to explain each of these aims in the exam.

1 Punishment

The aim of a retributive sentence is to punish the offender. The phrase 'an eye for an eye, a tooth for a tooth' is often used when discussing this aim. The idea is that if a person has knowingly done wrong, he or she deserves to be punished and society expects this.

Another form of punishment is denunciation. This is where society expresses its outrage at the behaviour of the individual and condemns it. This is sometimes used in the USA where convicted shop-lifters are made to stand outside the shop that they stole from with a sign proclaiming that they are thieves. Local newspapers also feature sections 'naming and shaming' those who have been convicted.

A controversial form of denunciation is the 'naming and shaming' of paedophiles. This occurs in some American states and is known as 'Megan's Law', named after a young girl murdered by a paedophile. A similar law may be introduced in England and Wales and would be called 'Sarah's Law' after 10-year-old Sarah Payne who was murdered in 2000.

2 Reduction of crime (deterrence)

The aim is to punish criminals in order to deter people from offending and thus reduce the number of offences committed. There are two different types of deterrence:
- A **specific deterrent** applies to an individual and the aim is to deter that particular person from re-offending.
- A sentence designed to act as a **general deterrent** is aimed at people in general.

The hope is that people will be deterred from committing crimes by the level of punishment that they will receive if convicted. This might be used if a particular type of crime has become prevalent, for example football hooliganism, joyriding or mobile phone robberies.

3 Rehabilitation

An offender is helped to solve the issues that lie behind his or her criminal behaviour. The intention is that if the problems are solved then the offender will avoid committing further offences. A drug addict who steals to fund his or her habit may be assisted to overcome his or her addiction, thereby removing the need to steal in future. A person who reacts aggressively and commits acts of violence may be sent on an 'anger management' course. Other offenders may be helped to develop their social skills and some may undertake training to improve their chances of employment.

4 Protection of the public

This is frequently used as a strong general justification for punishment and imprisonment in particular. It is argued that the public needs protection from dangerous criminals and prison removes these criminals from the public domain by restricting their liberty. In physically restraining offenders, it protects members of the public, albeit temporarily, from becoming the victims of further acts of crime.

5 Reparation

This is based on the notion that the offender 'makes amends' for his or her crime. The offender attempts to 'repair' the damage caused by the offence, usually by carrying out work in the community or by paying financial compensation. This encourages offenders to accept responsibility for their crimes.

B Types of sentence: adults

1 Custodial sentence

This is the most severe form of punishment and is reserved for serious offences.

As there is no longer the death penalty in the UK, the most severe criminal sanction for those over 21 is imprisonment. The punishment is the removal of the offender's liberty but can often go beyond this as prisoners' whole lives are affected. They may lose their jobs, homes and families as a result of a prison sentence.

Under the **Criminal Justice Act 2003**, the court can only pass a custodial sentence if it thinks that the offence was so serious that neither a fine alone nor a community sentence can be justified for it. It may also be imposed to protect the public from violent or sex offenders.

Make sure that you can give examples of crimes with mandatory and minimum sentences.

1.1 Mandatory/minimum sentence

Some offences have a mandatory sentence, e.g. the only sentence that can be passed for murder is life imprisonment. The **Powers of Criminal Courts (Sentencing) Act 2000** also lays down minimum sentences for some crimes. Unless the court thinks it unjust, a person will receive a minimum sentence of 7 years for a third class-A drug trafficking offence and a minimum of 3 years for a third conviction of domestic burglary.

1.2 Length of time served

It is rare for a prisoner to serve his or her full sentence. Usually, those sentenced to less than 4 years will be released after serving half of their sentence. Those with a longer sentence will have to serve two thirds of their sentence prior to release. When they are released, they remain on licence for the remainder of their sentence. Those sentenced to life may apply for parole once they have served the recommended tariff, but if released they will remain on licence for life.

1.3 Suspended sentence

In exceptional circumstances a person may receive a suspended prison sentence varying in length from 6 months to 2 years. This means that he or she does not have to go to prison. The sentence may be suspended for a period between 1 and 2 years. The offender is obliged to carry out work in the community and must not commit any further offences during the time the sentence is suspended, otherwise he or she will have to serve the sentence in prison.

At the end of January 2006 the Home Office statistics showed that the UK prison population was 75,661, made up of 71,305 males and 4,356 females. Each year, about 7% of those convicted receive prison sentences.

The HM Prison Service website is a good source of information (**www. hmprisonservice.gov. uk**) and includes a virtual prison tour.

2 Community sentence

The advantage of a community sentence is that it can be tailored to the needs of the individual.

A community sentence is imposed in 13% of cases each year. It is still a serious punishment but is an alternative to prison. Anyone aged 16 or over can be given a community sentence and it is seen as more effective at rehabilitating offenders than sending them to prison. Under s.148 of the **Criminal Justice Act 2003**, it can only be passed if the offence is serious enough to warrant it. Community sentences can be made up of various elements to ensure that they fit the needs of a particular defendant. They may include:

- between 40 and 300 hours of unpaid work in the community, such as cleaning graffiti or collecting charity-bag donations
- supervision by the probation service
- treatment for drug or alcohol addiction
- anger, alcohol or drug training programmes that look at an offender's behaviour
- an activity requirement obliging the offender to undertake an activity for a set number of days
- prohibited activity requirement banning the offender from certain activities
- a curfew requiring an offender to remain in a specified place at certain times

3 Fine

A fine requires the offender to pay a financial penalty and may be imposed alone or in addition to another type of sentence. Magistrates can give a maximum fine of £5,000 but there is no maximum amount in the Crown Court. When setting the level of a fine, the court must take into account two factors: first, the seriousness of the offence and second, the financial means of the offender, as the offender may go to prison if the fine is not paid. According to the Home Office, fines are imposed in approximately 71% of cases each year, making them by far the most common type of sentence.

4 Discharge

Discharge is imposed in 8% of cases, when the defendant has been convicted of an offence but the court is of the opinion that punishment is unnecessary for some reason. There are two different types of discharge — conditional and absolute. A **conditional discharge** means that although the offender will have a criminal record, no further action will be taken against him or her, as long as he or she does not commit a further offence within a specified time period of up to 3 years. If the offender does commit a further offence, he or she may be re-sentenced for this offence as well as receiving whatever sentence is passed for the second offence. An **absolute discharge** means that the offender will have a criminal record but no further action is taken against him or her.

C Types of sentence: young offenders

A young offender is anyone under 18 years old who commits a crime. Many of the sentences given to young offenders are the same as those imposed upon adults. Youths can receive conditional and absolute discharges as well as fines. There are differences, however, between community and custodial sentences given to adults and those given to youths.

In the exam you may be required to describe each type of sentence available.

1 Custodial sentences

Offenders under 18 cannot be given a custodial sentence but they may be detained elsewhere, for example in a young offenders' institution or local authority accommodation.

1.1 Detention and training order

Detention and training orders can be given to those aged between 12 and 17 and sentences them to custody for a period of between 4 months and 2 years. It is a serious punishment and is usually only given to those who have a history of offending. The first half of the sentence is spent in custody while the second half is spent in the community under the supervision of the Youth Offending Team.

1.2 Detention under sections 90 and 91 Powers of Criminal Courts (Sentencing) Act 2000

This applies when a young offender is convicted of an offence for which an adult could receive at least 14 years in custody and can only be passed in the Crown Court. A murder conviction falls under s.90, and all other crimes are covered by s.91. The youth will be kept in custody for any time up to the maximum limit that an adult convicted of the same crime could receive.

1.3 Sentence less than 4 years

If the offender is given a sentence of less than 4 years, he or she will be released at the half-way point and will then be under supervision up to the point at which three quarters of the sentence has passed. Some might be released earlier and monitored via tagging.

1.4 Sentence of 4 years or more

If the offender is given a sentence of 4 years or more, he or she will attend a parole hearing and, if successful, leave custody at the half-way point of the sentence. If the offender is unsuccessful, he or she will leave at the two-thirds point. In either case, the offender will be kept under supervision until three quarters of the sentence has passed.

2 Community sentences

2.1 Reparation order

Reparation orders are intended to help young offenders understand the consequences of their offending and take responsibility for their behaviour. Offenders must try to repair the harm caused by their offence. If the victim agrees, he or she may have direct contact with the offender. Otherwise, the offender repays the community as a whole — usually by carrying out work such as cleaning graffiti.

2.2 Referral order

If the young offender is in court for the first time and pleads guilty, he or she may be given a referral order. This requires attendance at a Youth Offender Panel, which is made up of two volunteers from the local community and someone from the Youth Offending Team. The young offender, his or her parents, the panel and sometimes the victim, all agree upon a contract aimed at repairing the damage that the offending has caused and minimising the risk of re-offending.

2.3 Attendance centre order

The young person is required to go to an attendance centre for a certain number of hours, usually spread over Saturday mornings. These centres are run by the police and include activities that centre on discipline, physical training and social skills.

2.4 Action plan order

An action plan order lasts 3 months and is a programme individually tailored to address the specific underlying causes of the young offender in question. It aims

to rehabilitate the offender and may involve activities focused on reparation, going to an attendance centre or undertaking educational programmes.

2.5 Supervision order

Supervision orders apply to offenders aged between 10 and 16 years and involve close supervision by social services or the probation service for up to 3 years. A range of conditions can be attached to the order, including curfews or residence requirements.

2.6 Community rehabilitation order

For those aged between 16 and 17, this sentence is equivalent to a supervision order. It is supervised by a Youth Offending Team.

2.7 Community punishment order

This can only be passed for those aged 16 to 17 years and requires completion of unpaid work within the community for a specified number of hours (between 40 and 240).

D Sentencing practice

> An understanding of how courts decide what sentences to give will greatly assist you with this topic.

In the Magistrates' Court the magistrates decide on the sentence while at the Crown Court the judge sentences the offender. Additionally, under the **Powers of Criminal Courts (Sentencing) Act 2000**, the magistrates may send a convicted offender to the Crown Court to be sentenced if they feel that their powers of sentencing are not sufficient — magistrates have the power to pass a sentence of up to 12 months' imprisonment for a summary offence.

Pre-sentence report

As mentioned above, the courts may order a pre-sentence report to be prepared by the probation service before proceeding to sentence. The offender meets with a probation officer who then prepares the report. Each report contains basic information such as the offender's age and background, and details any previous convictions. Additionally, it includes details of the offender's attitude to the offence as well as details of the offence itself. The report may also include the views of the victim. The offender is assessed as to the risk of his or her re-offending and whether he or she is considered to be a danger to the public. On the basis of this information, a type of sentence is recommended.

> The courts may choose not to follow the recommendations in the report.

Tariff system

Courts often employ a tariff system to determine an appropriate sentence. The idea is that the punishment should fit the crime and that those committing similar offences should receive similar sentences. Sentencing guidelines are issued to the courts by the Sentencing Guidelines Council. The aim of the guidelines is to help to achieve consistency in sentencing. Courts are given a guideline sentence for an

offence of a particular type, and they then consider any aggravating and mitigating factors before deciding upon the actual sentence.

2.1 Aggravating factors

Aggravating factors are likely to lead to a longer sentence.

These are factors that make an offence more serious and can result in a more severe sentence being passed. They can include a number of considerations, such as: if a weapon was used; if the attack was premeditated; if the offence involved a breach of trust; if there was a racist or religious motive behind the offence; or if the victim was particularly vulnerable. They also include any relevant previous convictions.

2.2 Mitigating factors

Mitigating factors are likely to lead to a shorter sentence.

The court takes mitigating factors into account, which may mean that the offender receives a more lenient sentence than he or she would have done if these were not present. Mitigating factors may relate to the offender and can include previous good character, personal circumstances and the fact that he or she has shown remorse. A prompt guilty plea can reduce the sentence by up to 20%. Other mitigating factors include: assisting the police; the fact that the offence was committed on the spur of the moment rather that being premeditated; the fact that the offender was provoked; or an attempt by the offender to compensate the victim.

Summary of Topic 11

Aims of sentencing

1 **Retribution:** the aim of a retributive sentence is to punish the offender. The phrase 'an eye for an eye, a tooth for a tooth' is often used when discussing this aim. The idea is that if a person has knowingly done wrong, he or she deserves to be punished and society expects this.

2 **Rehabilitation:** an offender is helped to solve the issues that lie behind his or her criminal behaviour.

3 **Reparation:** this is based on the notion that the offender 'makes amends' for his or her crime.

4 **Deterrence:** the aim is to punish criminals in order to deter people from offending and thus reduce the number of offences committed. There are two different types of deterrence: specific and general.

5 **Denunciation:** society expresses its outrage at the behaviour of the individual and condemns it.

6 **Protection of the public:** this removes these criminals from the public domain by restricting their liberty.

Types of sentence: adults

1 **Custodial sentence:** the most severe criminal sanction for those over 21 is imprisonment.

   a **Mandatory/minimum sentence:** some offences have a mandatory sentence, e.g. the only sentence that can be passed for murder is life imprisonment. The **Powers of Criminal Courts (Sentencing) Act 2000** also lays down minimum sentences for some crimes.

   b **Length of time served:** usually, those sentenced to less than 4 years will be released after serving half of their sentence. Those with a longer sentence will have to serve two thirds of their sentence prior to release. When they are released, they remain on licence for the remainder of their sentence.

   c **Suspended sentence:** in exceptional circumstances a person may receive a suspended prison sentence, varying in length from 6 months to 2 years.

2 **Community sentence:** community sentences can be made up of various elements to ensure that they fit the needs of a particular defendant. They may include between 40 and 300 hours of unpaid work in the community such as cleaning graffiti or collecting charity-bag donations. Other elements include supervision by the probation service, treatment for drug or alcohol addiction treatment, or anger, alcohol or drug training programmes.

3 **Fine:** a fine requires the offender to pay a financial penalty and may be imposed alone or in addition to another type of sentence. Magistrates can give a maximum fine of £5,000, but there is no maximum amount in the Crown Court.

4 **Discharge:** discharge is granted in cases where the defendant has been convicted of an offence but the court is of the opinion that punishment is unnecessary for some reason. There are two different types — conditional and absolute.

Types of sentence: young offenders

A young offender is anyone under 18 years old who commits a crime. Many of the sentences given to young offenders are the same as those imposed upon adults. Youths can receive conditional and absolute discharges as well as fines. There are differences, however, between community and custodial sentences given to adults and those given to youths.

Sentencing practice

1 **Pre-sentence report:** the probation service suggests a suitable sentence after considering the circumstances of the case.

2 **Tariff system:** courts often employ this system to determine an appropriate sentence. The idea is that the punishment should fit the crime and that those committing similar offences should receive similar sentences. Sentencing guidelines are issued to the courts by the Sentencing Guidelines Council.

a **Aggravating factors:** these are factors that make an offence more serious and can result in a more severe sentence being passed. They can include a number of things such as if a weapon was used, if the attack was premeditated, if the offence involved a breach of trust, if there was a racist or religious motive behind the offence, or if the victim was particularly vulnerable. It also includes any relevant previous convictions. Aggravating factors are likely to lead to a longer sentence.

b **Mitigating factors:** the court takes these into account and they may mean that the offender receives a more lenient sentence than he or she would have done if these were not present. Mitigating factors may relate to the offender and can include previous good character, personal circumstances and the fact that he or she has shown remorse. A prompt guilty plea can reduce the sentence by up to 20%. Other mitigating factors include: assisting the police; the fact that the offence was committed on the spur of the moment rather that being premeditated; the fact that the offender was provoked; or an attempt by the offender to compensate the victim.

Lawyers in the British legal system are split into two branches: barristers and solicitors. Both have different routes to qualification, differing roles and separate governing bodies. This division stems from the nineteenth century and the twin monopolies that the professions held over the types of work that they could undertake. Under these monopolies, solicitors had exclusive rights to conduct litigation and to carry out conveyancing, while barristers monopolised rights of audience in the higher courts. Debates have raged over the need for two branches of the legal profession and indeed, changes have been made, most notably by the **Courts and Legal Services Act 1990**. Solicitors no longer have exclusive rights over the conduct of litigation as barristers can be approached directly in some circumstances. Additionally, solicitors can now gain higher rights of audience as barristers have lost their exclusive right to advocacy in the higher courts. As well as solicitors and barristers, there are other groups working in the British legal system, including legal executives, who carry out similar work to solicitors.

A Barristers

1 Training

1.1 Law degree

Potential barristers will usually have completed a degree. This is usually in law but may be in another subject area. There are many qualifying law degrees but all cover the foundation subjects, which are contract law, tort, public law (including constitutional law, administrative law and human rights law), criminal law, property law, equity and trusts, and European Union law.

1.2 Graduate Diploma in Law

If the degree is not in law, candidates have to undertake the Graduate Diploma in Law (GDL). If undertaken full time, it is a year-long course that covers the same foundation subjects as a law degree.

1.3 Bar Vocational Course

The next stage of training is the Bar Vocational Course (BVC), lasting 1 year full time or 2 years part time. The course covers skills such as case preparation, criminal and civil litigation, advocacy, opinion writing, ethics and evidence.

1.4 Inns of Court

Potential barristers must join one of the four Inns of Court — either Gray's Inn, Lincoln's Inn, Inner Temple or Middle Temple — which are all based in London. Prior to the existence of the BVC, the Inns were a way for students to interact with and learn from other barristers. Today, students still have a chance to interact with other barristers as they must dine at their Inn 12 times before being called

Have a look on the internet at different law degrees to see what areas they cover.

Candidates have to pay several thousand pounds in fees for this course and it adds an extra year onto their study.

Competition for places on the BVC is intense.

to the Bar. The Inns also provide scholarships, law libraries, accommodation for barristers' chambers and can discipline barristers if a complaint is made against them.

1.5 Pupillage

Pupillage is a type of apprenticeship and is usually carried out in a barristers' chambers. It is usually divided into two periods of 6 months. A pupil will shadow an experienced barrister for 6 months and then undertake his or her own work in the second 6 months. There are a limited number of other places where pupillage can be carried out, including working in the European Commission. Competition for pupillages is fierce and many of those who have completed the BVC will not gain a pupillage.

1.6 Tenancy

Once pupillage is completed, the barrister needs to become a permanent member of a chambers, or a 'tenant'. Tenancy is notoriously difficult to find and barristers often have to spend time as a 'squatter' in the chambers where they did their pupillage before moving on elsewhere. Most of those who complete a pupillage will not find a tenancy.

1.7 Continuing professional development

Barristers must keep accurate records to demonstrate that they have undertaken the necessary hours.

Even after qualification, barristers must undertake continuing professional development (CPD). They must complete a minimum of 45 hours of CPD within the first 3 years of practice. This ongoing training covers advocacy, case preparation and procedure, professional conduct and ethics.

2 *Work*

There are about 15,000 barristers who are governed and supervised by the Bar Council. Most of these barristers are self-employed but share administrative costs by working together in chambers. A few are sole practitioners and some are employed by various companies and organisations.

2.1 Advocacy

Advocacy means speaking on behalf of someone else.

Traditionally, barristers have specialised in advocacy — representing clients in court in both criminal and civil cases.

2.2 Conferences

Barristers also have conferences with their clients to discuss certain aspects of their cases. These conferences may be before the case goes to court, or in straightforward cases a barrister may hold a pre-hearing conference on the actual day of the court hearing.

Often a client does not meet his or her barrister until the morning of the hearing.

2.3 Opinions

Barristers also write opinions, usually on the instructions of a solicitor. Opinions give their views on matters such as the strengths and weaknesses of a case, how

a complex area of the law relates to a particular case and whether evidence is likely to be admissible or not.

2.4 The 'cab-rank' rule

Self-employed barristers work according to the 'cab-rank' rule, whereby if they have the time and skills and are offered a reasonable fee then they must accept the job. This is to avoid situations where some people may not be able to get a barrister to represent them.

2.5 Instructing a barrister

It used to be the case that only solicitors could instruct a barrister but from 1989, some professions were allowed to instruct barristers directly, either for their own needs or on behalf of their clients. Barristers can provide direct assistance but those seeking such access have to apply for a licence. Those who are licensed include members of organisations such as the Chartered Institute of Building, the Society of Financial Advisors, the Engineering Council and several accountancy institutes. Some groups have direct access without the need for a licence, including employed barristers and certain legal advice centres.

2.6 Public access

Members of the public can, since 2003, go directly to a barrister in a number of cases, rather than needing to instruct a solicitor first. This is known as public access. Barristers must fulfil certain conditions before they can accept public access work, including practising for at least 3 years and attending a training course. Public access is allowed in most areas but there are exceptions, which include some areas of criminal, family and immigration work. Some barristers may not accept any public access work but if they do, they must consider whether it is in the interests of the client and the interests of justice for the case to proceed on these grounds.

2.7 Employed barristers

About 3,000 barristers are employed rather than self-employed. They work for a variety of organisations including in-house legal departments, government departments and advice centres.

2.8 Queen's Counsel (QC)

Some barristers may apply to become a Queen's Counsel. The system dealing with these applications has recently changed and has become more transparent than previous methods, which had been heavily criticised. Applicants pay a fee of £1,800 initially and a further £2,250 if successful. They complete a form giving details of their work and skills and listing several referees who are familiar with their work. After a selection panel has reviewed their application, candidates are interviewed. The advantages for those that are successful are that they gain an elevated status among their peers. They can command much higher fees, often as well as having a junior barrister to assist them. Additionally, they can wear silk rather than polyester gowns!

3 The Bar Council

The Bar Council was formed in 1894 as the governing body for barristers. Today, made up of about 115 barristers, its purpose is to represent the interests of the Bar and oversee training and qualification of barristers and it meets several times a year. Since 2006 the new Bar Standards Board has taken over responsibility for regulation. It has a membership of 15, about half of whom are lay people.

4 Regulation

Sometimes clients may be unhappy with the services of a barrister. Clients with a complaint against a barrister should speak to their solicitor, if they have one, to see if the solicitor agrees with the complaint and if he or she can resolve it. In most cases the matter can be resolved at this stage. If not, however, the client has two options — to use the disciplinary process or to take the barrister to court.

4.1 The Bar Council

If the complaint has not been resolved, the next step is for the client to contact the Bar Council. This must usually be done within 6 months of the complaint arising.

4.2 The Complaints Commissioner

The Complaints Commissioner oversees the complaints process and investigates any complaints. The current commissioner is Michael Scott, who is a non-lawyer entirely independent from the Bar Council. If, after consideration of the complaint, the commissioner thinks that it might be justified, he will refer it to the Professional Conduct and Complaints Committee (PCC) for its opinion.

4.3 The Professional Conduct and Complaints Committee

The PCC will assess the nature of the complaint. The complaint may be about professional misconduct, such as leaving a case at short notice without good reason or acting against a client's interests. If so, the Bar Council can give advice, order the barrister to repay fees, suspend the barrister or even disbar the barrister so that he or she can no longer practice. If the complaint is about inadequate service, such as delay or rudeness towards the client, the Bar Council can require a barrister to apologise, repay fees or pay up to £5,000 in compensation. Some complaints might involve elements of professional misconduct and inadequate service.

If the PCC agrees with the Complaints Commissioner and considers that the complaint may be justified, the complaint is sent to a disciplinary panel. The panel makes a final decision as to whether the complaint is justified and, if so, to determine the measures that should be taken.

4.4 Legal Services Ombudsman

If the client is unhappy with the way that the Bar Council investigated its complaint, he or she can make a final appeal to the Legal Services Ombudsman. The process is the same for barristers and solicitors (see below).

4.5 Action through the courts

As with solicitors (see below), a dissatisfied client can also sue the barrister through the courts for negligence. Barristers used to have immunity from liability but that changed in 2000 when the House of Lords abolished this protection in the case of *Arthur J. S. Hall and Co.* v *Simons* (2000).

B Solicitors

1 Training

1.1 Law degree/GDL

Like barristers, solicitors will usually have completed a degree. Again, this is usually in law but may be in another subject area, in which case, as with barristers, they have to undertake the Graduate Diploma in Law (GDL). The GDL is the same course whether the candidate is an aspiring barrister or a would-be solicitor.

1.2 Legal practice course

> If answering a question on training, give examples of the types of areas studied on the LPC.

This vocational course lasts 1 year full time or 2 years part time. It provides practical skills such as problem solving, accounts, drafting, advising, ethics and legal research.

1.3 Training contract

After having passed the LPC, the potential solicitor must find a training contract. This is usually 2 years' full-time practical experience in a solicitor's office but it can also be with a government department, the Crown Prosecution Service, the Magistrates' Court Service or in-house legal departments. The trainee's time is usually spent working in various departments so that he or she gains practical experience in at least three different areas as stipulated by the Law Society, which regulates all training contracts. Training contracts are usually organised so that a trainee spends about 6 months each in four different departments, although trainees may instead work in a variety of areas on a daily basis during the 2 years.

> Some firms will pay GDL and LPC fees. Look at recruitment brochures or websites to find out how to apply for training contracts with different firms and what they are looking for in potential trainees.

Throughout the training contract the trainee is supervised by an experienced solicitor and the trainee's performance is reviewed on a regular basis. The Law Society requires that trainee solicitors are paid a minimum salary, as prescribed by it, and the salary level is reviewed annually. As of August 2005, the minimum salaries are £16,450 for trainees working in Central London and £14,720 for trainees working elsewhere, although many firms pay much more than this. Competition for training contracts is fierce and many firms recruit up to 2 years in advance. After completion of the training contract the firm usually employs the trainee as a salaried solicitor, as long as a vacancy is available.

1.4 Continuing professional development

Solicitors must continue to develop their skills and to keep them updated by completing a minimum of 16 hours of CPD each year. Much of this takes the form

of courses accredited by the Law Society but can also include legal writing, research and work shadowing. All CPD should be recorded and a failure to complete the necessary number of hours may result in disciplinary procedures administered by the Law Society.

2 Work

There are over 100,000 solicitors who are supervised and represented by the Law Society. There is much diversity among them in terms of the work that they do.

Some solicitors work alone but most tend to work in partnerships, owned and managed by several partners who take a share of any profits. Solicitors' offices also employ salaried solicitors who are paid a fixed amount each month. Most salaried solicitors will be aiming to be a partner one day but this can take many years.

The type of work that a solicitor might do varies greatly depending upon the type of firm that he or she works for. In addition, most solicitors specialise in a couple of areas and may know little about the law in other areas.

2.1 Types of law firm

Visit the websites of various firms of solicitors to gain a better understanding of the different types of firm.

Most law firms fall into one of two categories — high street firms and commercial firms.

High street firms generally deal with individual clients and cover criminal law or civil law or both. Some will carry out publicly funded work paid for by legal aid. High street firms may have several offices throughout a region. They may advise and represent a client who has been charged with a criminal offence. They may carry out the necessary conveyancing when someone is buying or selling property or they may advise on personal injury matters or the mechanics of drafting a will.

Commercial firms tend to work for businesses rather than individuals and as such are called on to provide a different range of services. They often have offices throughout the world. Commercial firms may advise clients on intellectual property matters, mergers and acquisitions, employment contracts and business conveyancing. Commercial lawyers may also represent wealthy individuals.

2.2 Working day

As there is so much variation in the type of work solicitors carry out, there is a big difference in the activities that make up their typical working day. Many solicitors begin by reviewing and responding to the huge amount of mail that they receive. Some will draft documents such as a contract of employment or a will. Many solicitors spend their days meeting with clients or negotiating settlements or attending court. Others may draft instructions for a barrister whose opinion they require upon a particular matter. All solicitors record the amount of time spent on a particular matter and then charge their clients accordingly.

2.3 Employed solicitors

Not all solicitors work in private practice. Increasing numbers of solicitors are employed outside solicitors' firms. They may work in an in-house legal department

for a large corporation. They may work for the Legal Services Commission or the Crown Prosecution Service, for local government or in the Magistrates' Courts as a clerk.

3 The Law Society

Set up in 1842, the Law Society works to represent the interests of solicitors. Its role includes overseeing training and qualifications and ensuring that those carrying out publicly funded work are receiving adequate payment. Since 2006, regulatory matters have become the responsibility of the Regulation Board — made up of lay people and solicitors.

4 Regulation

You may be asked to describe this procedure or the equivalent process for barristers in an exam question, so make sure that you know it — draw a flow-chart to help with understanding.

There are various ways to complain about a solicitor if a client is dissatisfied with the service that he or she has received or the amount that he or she has been asked to pay.

4.1 Contacting the solicitor

The first step is to raise the matter with the solicitor or the firm that he or she works for. All firms should have a process in place for dealing with complaints. Ideally, this should be done in writing — the Law Society even has a resolution form that can be printed off and filled in via its website. The dissatisfied client should explain what the complaint is about and how he or she wishes it to be resolved. Many complaints are resolved at this stage.

4.2 The Law Society

If the firm does not reply within a reasonable amount of time or if the complaint has not been resolved, the next step is for the client to contact the Law Society. This must be within the time limits that it sets down — usually 6 months. The Law Society will investigate the complaint and has the power to reduce the solicitor's bill, order the solicitor to pay compensation of up to £15,000 or tell him or her to correct the mistake and meet any costs incurred. The Office of the Legal Services Complaints Commissioner was set up following the **Access to Justice Act 1999**. It works with the Law Society and represents the interests of consumers to improve complaints handling.

4.3 Legal Services Ombudsman

If the client is unhappy with the way that the Law Society investigated the complaint, he or she can make a final appeal to the Legal Services Ombudsman (LSO), currently Zahida Manzoor. This must be within 3 months of receiving the Law Society's decision. The LSO will not usually look at the original complaint but rather at how it was dealt with by the Law Society. The powers of the LSO include recommending that the Law Society reconsider the complaint, formally criticising the Law Society or ordering it to pay compensation.

4.4 Action through the courts

A dissatisfied client can also sue the solicitor through the courts for negligence. He or she would have to prove that the solicitor's work fell below the standards of that of a reasonable solicitor. The courts are able to award compensation if the client is successful.

Summary of Topic 12

Barristers

1 **Training:** requirements are a law degree or other degree and GDL, completing a BVC and gaining membership of one of the Inns of Court, gaining a pupillage, gaining tenancy at a chambers and undertaking continuing professional development.
2 **Work:** this includes advocacy, conferences, opinions, the 'cab-rank' rule, instructing a barrister, and limited public access. Most barristers are self-employed but a few are employed by big businesses and organisations.
3 **The Bar Council:** its purpose is to represent the interests of the Bar and oversee the training and qualification of barristers. It meets several times a year.
4 **Regulation:** clients with a complaint against a barrister should speak to their solicitor, if they have one, to see if the solicitor agrees with the complaint and if he or she can resolve it. In most cases the matter can be resolved at this stage, but if not, the client has two options — to use the disciplinary process or to take the barrister to court (via the Bar Council, the Complaints Commissioner, the Professional Conduct and Complaints Committee and the Legal Services Ombudsman). Barristers used to have immunity from liability but that changed in 2000 when the House of Lords abolished this protection in the case of *Arthur J. S. Hall and Co.* v *Simons* (2000).

Solicitors

1 **Training:** requirements are a law degree or other degree and GDL, passing a legal practice course, finding a training contract and taking continuing professional development.
2 **Work:** the type of work that a solicitor might do varies greatly depending upon the type of firm that he or she works for. In addition, most solicitors specialise in a couple of areas and may know little about the law in other areas.
3 **The Law Society:** the Law Society works to represent the interests of solicitors.
4 **Regulation:** there are various ways to complain about a solicitor if a client is dissatisfied with the service that he or she has received or the amount that he or she has been asked to pay: contact the solicitor, the Law Society, the Legal Services Ombudsman or action through the courts.

A The role of judges

Judges fulfil an essential role in any legal system. Their job is to ensure that the law is applied fairly and correctly. Judges also play a role in making law, which is done through precedent and statutory interpretation. Once the lawyers have prepared the cases, they are argued in front of the judge, whose role will depend on the type of case before him or her. In criminal cases, judges must ensure that the jury understands the law that it is being asked to apply. The judge must also pass an appropriate sentence when required. In civil law, where the use of juries is much reduced, cases are often heard by a judge alone and it is the judge who decides on both the law and the facts. Whatever the type of case, judges must ensure that they remain independent and impartial at all times.

A common theme of exam questions is to ask for a description of the selection process and qualifications required for the various judicial posts.

B Types of judge

As with the courts, judges are arranged in a hierarchical structure and thus there are different types of judges who hear different types of cases in the various courts.

1 Lord Chief Justice of England and Wales

As of 3 April 2006, the Lord Chief Justice took over from the Lord Chancellor as the head of the judiciary. The Lord Chief Justice is also the President of the Courts. The current holder of the post is Lord Phillips of Worth Matravers. The role carries over 400 duties, but the main ones include the training and guidance of judges, representing the judiciary in Parliament, giving judgements in important cases, dealing with complaints against judges and chairing the Sentencing Guidelines Council, which issues guidelines to courts as to appropriate sentencing practice. The next Lord Chief Justice will be appointed by the Judicial Appointments Commission and will probably be selected from the Appeal Court judges. The candidate could also be selected from among the Law Lords.

2 Master of the Rolls

Next, in terms of judicial importance, is the Master of the Rolls, who is the leading judge in civil matters in the Court of Appeal and is president of its Civil Division.

The Master of the Rolls authorises solicitors to practise and deals with their professional rules. He or she is also consulted on any relevant matters, including practice and procedure in the civil justice system as a whole. Appointments are made by the Queen, on the recommendation of the prime minister, who in turn is advised by the Lord Chancellor after consultation with senior members of the judiciary.

3 Superior judges

3.1 Law Lords

Title: Lords of Appeal in Ordinary/Law Lords

Number: 12

Court: House of Lords and Privy Council

Appointed by: the Queen, on the recommendation of the prime minister, who has been advised by the Lord Chancellor

Qualifications: appointed from those who hold high judicial office, e.g. a judge in the Court of Appeal, or from those with 15 years' experience of Supreme Courts

3.2 Judges in the Court of Appeal

Title: Lord and Lady Justices of Appeal

Number: 37

Court: Court of Appeal

Appointed by: the Queen, on the recommendation of the prime minister, who has been advised by the Lord Chancellor; the Lord Chancellor will have consulted senior members of the judiciary

Qualifications: the statutory qualification is a 10-year High Court qualification or being a High Court judge; most Court of Appeal judges are promoted from the ranks of experienced High Court judges

3.3 High Court judges

Title: Mr or Mrs Justice (Surname)

Number: 112

Courts: High Court and serious cases in Crown Court

Appointed by: the Queen, on the advice of the Lord Chancellor

Qualifications: must have had a right of audience in relation to all proceedings in the High Court for 10 years or have been a circuit judge for at least 2 years; once appointed, they are assigned to a division of the High Court — the Chancery Division, Queen's Bench Division or Family Division

4 Inferior judges

4.1 Circuit judges

Number: 636, and 42 deputy circuit judges who sit part time in retirement

Courts: circuit judges are assigned to a particular circuit and may sit at any of the Crown and County Courts on that circuit. They can hear both criminal and civil cases

Appointed by: the Queen, on the recommendation of the Lord Chancellor

Qualifications: 10-year Crown Court or 10-year County Court qualification or to have been the holder of one of a number of other judicial offices for at least 3 years

4.2 District judges

Number: 412, and 744 deputy district judges

Courts: on appointment, a district judge is assigned to a particular circuit and may sit at any of the County Courts or District Registries of the High Court in that circuit; a District Registry is part of the High Court situated in various places in England and Wales

4.3 District judges (Magistrates' Court)

Number: 128, and 167 deputy district judges (Magistrates' Court)

Court: district judges (Magistrates' Courts) hear cases in Magistrates' Courts; they are paid and deal with the full range of cases and usually hear the longest and most complicated cases; they can either sit alone or with lay magistrates

Appointed by: the Lord Chancellor

Qualifications: 7-year general qualification

4.4 Recorders (part-time judges)

Number: 1,404

Courts: recorders may sit in both the Crown and County Courts; most begin in the Crown Court, although after about 2 years and further training they may sit in the County Courts; a recorder must sit for at least 15 days a year, but not normally for more than 30 days

Appointed by: the Queen, on the recommendation of the Lord Chancellor

Qualifications: the statutory qualification for appointment as a recorder is a 10-year Crown Court or 10-year County Court qualification

C Appointments process

1 Judicial Appointments Commission

From April 2006 the Judicial Appointments Commission (JAC) has been responsible for the selection and recruitment of judges, which used to be the responsibility of the Lord Chancellor. Set up by the **Constitutional Reform Act 2005**, it is an independent body that selects candidates for judicial office. Once selected, the JAC's recommended candidates are appointed by the Queen or Lord Chancellor. The introduction of the JAC was designed to make the judicial appointments system more transparent, as it has been criticised in the past for being shrouded in secrecy. The JAC is made up of 15 commissioners, some of whom have a legal background — as members of the judiciary, lawyers or tribunals — while others, including the chairperson, are members of the public. The JAC produces an annual report and is accountable to the Lord Chancellor.

2 Applications

Adverts are placed in papers, legal journals and on the website of the Department for Constitutional Affairs for appointments up to and including High Court judge.

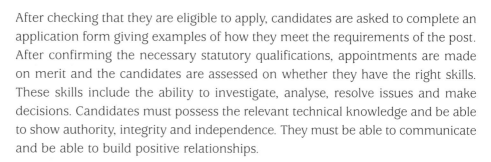

After checking that they are eligible to apply, candidates are asked to complete an application form giving examples of how they meet the requirements of the post. After confirming the necessary statutory qualifications, appointments are made on merit and the candidates are assessed on whether they have the right skills. These skills include the ability to investigate, analyse, resolve issues and make decisions. Candidates must possess the relevant technical knowledge and be able to show authority, integrity and independence. They must be able to communicate and be able to build positive relationships.

Judicial appointments beyond the High Court, in the Court of Appeal and House of Lords, are by invitation only and are not advertised.

3 Consultation

The next stage is that of consultation with people who are familiar with a candidate's work. Judges and other members of the legal profession are asked for their written comments, which will provide information on the candidate's suitability. The candidate may also nominate people to provide a reference. For senior appointments, the Lord Chancellor will always consult senior judges, including the Law Lords, for their views.

4 Sifts

Applications are considered and a shortlist of those most suitable is drawn up so that they may be invited for interview.

5 Interviews

Candidates are interviewed for about an hour and are questioned by a panel to test whether they have the necessary skills and experience. The panel will usually be made up of a member of the Department for Constitutional Affairs, a judicial member and a lay person. Sometimes a candidate may be required to complete a written exercise to test his or her skills or technical knowledge.

6 Assessment centre

For some roles, including deputy district judge (both civil and Magistrates' Courts), candidates will be invited to an assessment centre for a day instead of going through the interview stage. At the centre they will undertake a series of exercises, including role-plays and an interview, designed to test whether they have the necessary skills.

7 Successful applicants

The names of those who successfully demonstrate that they have the necessary attributes are passed to the Lord Chancellor, who considers their applications and then makes a final decision as to whether they should be appointed. Feedback is available to anyone who has not been successful to assist him or her with any future applications.

8 Training

Once judges have been selected they need to undergo initial training, which is the responsibility of the Judicial Studies Board. This body also oversees the training of magistrates (see below). Judges must attend an induction course and observe trials and case management in court. Criminal judges will visit prisons and young offenders' institutes. Training continues for all judges throughout their career and every 3 years, judges in the Crown, County and High Courts must attend a residential course to keep them informed of changes in both law and procedure.

D Removal and retirement

1 Removal

Because it is so difficult to remove them, judges are said to have 'security of tenure'.

It is difficult to remove a judge from his or her position. Circuit and district judges can be dismissed by the Lord Chancellor. Dismissal is on limited grounds but generally happens as a result of misbehaviour, such as failure to complete training requirements or repeated failure to meet sitting requirements. Those in the higher courts (High Court and above) are protected by the **Act of Settlement 1700**, which means that they can only be removed by the Queen following a petition of both Houses of Parliament. This has only ever been used once. Judges can also be removed due to incapacity.

2 Resignation

Judges may resign at any age.

3 Retirement

The usual age for retirement is 70.

E Judicial independence

It is important that judges are independent from pressure from government and other sources, not least to ensure that trials are fair and are seen to be so, but also because of the constitutional idea of the separation of powers. Under the doctrine of the separation of powers — a theory put forward by the French political thinker Montesquieu — state power should not be in the hands of just one person or group. According to the theory, power should be divided into three: the power to suggest law, the power to make law and the power to enforce law. In our system, the government has the power to suggest law, Parliament has the power to make it and judges enforce it. Each group acts independently and provides a check on the other two so that dictatorship and tyranny can be avoided. Judges should therefore be independent and this is achieved in various ways. Using judicial review (see Topic 2, 'Delegated legislation'), judges can decide whether a piece of

legislation is legal. The fact that it is so difficult to remove judges means that they cannot be pressurised by threat of redundancy and the fact that judicial salaries are not voted for by Parliament ensures that wages cannot be used as a bargaining tool. Judges are not allowed to sit in any case in which they have a personal interest (see *Re Pinochet*, 1999). Additionally, judges cannot be sued for decisions made and things done in their role as judge.

> ### *Re Pinochet* 1999
>
> The former Chilean dictator General Pinochet was allowed to appeal a decision made by the House of Lords on the grounds of bias. He was fighting a decision to extradite him so that he could face genocide and torture charges relating to the death of thousands of people when he took power in Chile. One of the judges in the case, Lord Hoffman, was a director of the human rights group Amnesty International, which campaigned for Pinochet to be extradited. It was decided that this judge could not have been seen to have judged fairly in the case because of those links. There was no suggestion that Lord Hoffman actually was biased, but Lord Browne-Wilkinson stated the basic principle that 'justice must not only be done but must be seen to be done'.

Judges are not wholly independent — the Law Lords sit in Parliament and the courts, which is a clear breach of the separation of powers. The government is taking steps to change this, however, by setting up a new supreme court. As Parliament is supreme, judges cannot question a validly enacted Act of Parliament and judges must ensure that such Acts are upheld.

Make sure that you are able to evaluate judicial independence and are familiar with ways in which judges are independent as well as ways in which their independence is compromised.

F Evaluation

Several criticisms have been made of the current judicial system.

1 Diversity

One of the major criticisms of the judiciary is that it does not reflect society — the vast majority of judges are white, old, male and middle-class. There has only ever been one female judge in the House of Lords. Just 8% of judges in the Appeal Court are women, rising to 10% in the High Court. More women are to be found at the lower end of the judicial scale but even there, they only make up about 20%. The judicial representation of ethnic minority groups is even lower as they make up around 2% of judges. The Lord Chancellor has introduced measures designed to encourage more women and members of ethnic minority groups to apply, but it will take many years for the effects of this to be seen.

2 Selection and appointment

Many critics disliked the way that judges were appointed before April 2006, when the Judicial Appointments Commission took over the selection of candidates for judicial office, as it used to be a far more secretive procedure and there were

suggestions that candidates were not picked on merit, but rather on the grounds of whether they fitted the traditional image of a judge, i.e. white males. The changes introduced were designed to make the system more transparent and much fairer, but it remains to be seen whether this has actually been achieved.

Summary of Topic 13

The role of judges

The job of judges is to ensure that the law is applied fairly and correctly. Judges also play a role in making law, which is done through precedent and statutory interpretation. Judges must also pass an appropriate sentence when required. In civil law, where the use of juries is much reduced, cases are often heard by a judge alone and it is the judge who decides on both the law and the facts. Whatever the type of case, judges must ensure that they remain independent and impartial at all times.

Types of judge

1 The **Lord Chief Justice of England and Wales** is the head of the judiciary and President of the Courts. The main duties include the training and guidance of judges, representing the judiciary in Parliament, giving judgements in important cases, dealing with complaints against judges and chairing the Sentencing Guidelines Council, which issues guidelines to courts as to appropriate sentencing practice.

2 The **Master of the Rolls** is the leading judge in civil matters in the Court of Appeal and is president of its Civil Division.

3 **Superior judges** include Law Lords (House of Lords), Lord Justices of Appeal (Court of Appeal) and High Court judges (High Court).

4 **Inferior judges** include circuit judges (Crown Court and County Court), district judges (County Court and Magistrates' Court) and recorders (part time at Crown Court and County Court).

Appointments process

1 The **Judicial Appointments Commission** is responsible for the selection and recruitment of judges.

2 **Applications** for the inferior courts are advertised and appointment is based on merit. Superior judges are appointed by invitation.

3 **Consultation** requires references from other members of the legal profession. The next stage is consultation with people who are familiar with a candidate's work. Judges and other members of the legal profession are asked for their written comments, which provide information on the candidate's suitability. The candidate may also nominate people to provide a reference for him or her. For senior appointments the Lord Chancellor always consults senior judges, including the Law Lords, for their views.

4 **Sifts:** a shortlist is drawn up.

5 **Interviews** of candidates are held for about an hour and they are questioned by a panel to test whether they have the necessary skills and experience.

6 For some roles, including deputy district judge (both civil and Magistrates' courts), candidates are invited to an **assessment centre** for a day instead of going through the interview stage.

7 **Successful applicants** are appointed.

8 Once judges have been selected they need to undergo initial **training**, which is the responsibility of the Judicial Studies Board.

Removal and retirement

1 **Removal:** it is difficult to remove a judge from his or her position. Circuit and district judges can be dismissed by the Lord Chancellor. Dismissal is on limited grounds but generally occurs as a result of misbehaviour, such as failure to complete training requirements or repeated failure to meet sitting requirements. Those in the higher courts (High Court and above) are protected by the **Act of Settlement 1700**, which means that they can only be removed by the Queen following a petition of both Houses of Parliament. This has only ever been used once. Judges can also be removed due to incapacity.

2 **Resignation:** judges may resign at any age.

3 **Retirement:** the usual age for retirement is 70.

Judicial independence

It is important that judges are independent from pressure from government and other sources, not least to ensure that trials are fair and are seen to be so, but also because of the constitutional idea of the separation of powers. Under the doctrine of the separation of powers — a theory put forward by the French political thinker Montesquieu — state power should not be in the hands of just one person or group. According to the theory, power should be divided into three: the power to suggest law, the power to make law and the power to enforce law.

Evaluation

Several criticisms have been made of the current judicial system, including diversity, and the selection and appointment of judges.

Lay people in this context are those who do not require formal legal qualifications to fulfil their role. In the UK legal system this covers magistrates and those undertaking jury service.

A Magistrates

There are about 30,000 lay magistrates in England and Wales who work as unpaid volunteers. They usually sit on a bench of three magistrates, made up of a chairperson and two wingers. Magistrates do not need legal qualifications as there is a qualified legal advisor (a clerk) on hand to advise on law and procedure. Magistrates' work is split between civil and criminal matters.

1 Eligibility

1.1 Age

Magistrates must be aged between 18 and 65 and are required to retire at the age of 70.

1.2 Nationality

Candidates need not be British nationals but must swear allegiance to the Queen.

1.3 Qualifications

No formal qualifications are required and it is not necessary to have any legal experience, as the legal advisor is available to advise the magistrates on the law. Candidates must demonstrate that they have the requisite personal qualities, especially the six key characteristics of good character:

- personal integrity and the respect and trust of others
- understanding and communication
- social awareness
- maturity and sound temperament
- sound judgement
- commitment and reliability

Potential magistrates must also be in good health and ensure that they can carry out the necessary duties.

1.4 Conflicting occupations

Some jobs are regarded as incompatible with the role of a magistrate. This is usually because they could give the impression that the magistracy is not completely impartial. The Lord Chancellor has discretion over whether to appoint those in these occupations but will not usually appoint those in the police (including civilian employees and special constables), members of the armed forces, traffic wardens, members of or candidates for election to any parliament or assembly, or any other occupations that could conflict with the role of a

A popular topic on exam questions is the selection and appointment of magistrates, so make sure that you learn the processes well.

magistrate. Additionally, the occupations of a candidate's spouse, partner or close relatives are also considered and if their occupation falls into the categories above, the application will probably be unsuccessful.

1.5 Bankruptcy

Anyone who is an undischarged bankrupt will not be appointed as a magistrate, based on the fact that the public is unlikely to have any confidence in him or her. If a candidate has previously been declared bankrupt, he or she must disclose full details of the circumstances.

1.6 Criminal convictions

Candidates with criminal convictions or civil court orders must declare these on their application form. The circumstances of the offence will be considered. Minor offences, for example petty motoring offences, are not usually an issue but serious offences or a number of lesser offences may lead to the candidate being rejected.

2 Role

2.1 Criminal matters

Over 95% of all criminal cases are dealt with by magistrates. They have jurisdiction in both the adult and the youth court. The youth court deals with offenders between the ages of 10 and 17. Magistrates decide on applications for bail and decide the facts and law in trials. If they find a defendant guilty, or the defendant pleads guilty, then they must pass an appropriate sentence. This can range from an absolute discharge to 12 months in prison for a single offence. Magistrates may also send certain defendants to the Crown Court for sentencing (see Topic 11, 'Sentencing').

Magistrates may also sit with a judge in the Crown Court. They hear appeals from Magistrates' Courts against conviction or sentence.

2.2 Civil matters

Magistrates also have a civil jurisdiction. They deal with those who have not paid their council tax or other fines. Additionally, some magistrates undergo further training in family matters. They can then deal with residence and contact orders regarding children.

2.3 Other duties

Specialist committees consider appeals against local authority licensing decisions. Magistrates may be called upon at any time to respond to requests for warrants for arrest and search.

3 Appointment process

3.1 Visit to Magistrates' Court

Before applying to become a magistrate, potential candidates are encouraged to visit their local Magistrates' Court to gain a better understanding of the role.

3.2 Application form

The candidate completes an application form. The information is checked to ensure that all eligibility criteria are fulfilled and that the candidate has provided evidence that he or she has the six key qualities.

3.3 Interview

Once the application form is checked and found to be in order, candidates are invited for a first interview. This is carried out by members of the Local Advisory Committee, made up of both magistrates and non-magistrates. Candidates are assessed to see whether they have the necessary attributes. If successful at the first interview, potential magistrates are invited to a second interview, where they may undertake role-plays and sentencing exercises.

3.4 Background checks

Background checks are made on all candidates prior to appointment.

3.5 Appointment

Candidates are recommended to the secretary of state and Lord Chancellor for appointment by Local Advisory Committees. These consist of local people, including some magistrates. In making their recommendations, these committees consider the suitability of candidates, the number of vacancies and the need to ensure that the composition of each bench broadly reflects the diversity of the community it serves. Suitable candidates are appointed by the secretary of state and Lord Chancellor on behalf of the Queen.

4 Training

Once appointed, magistrates must undergo initial training. This lasts about 3 days and may be held over a weekend. The new magistrate must make at least three court observations and visit a prison and a young offenders' institute. All new magistrates are given a mentor to assist them. The mentor will be an experienced magistrate from the local area whose role is to offer guidance and support.

After about a year, a further 2 days' training is undertaken, made up of group work, case studies, classroom-based and home learning, and discussion. Magistrates are encouraged throughout training to develop the necessary skills, including decision making, communication and problem solving. At around this time, magistrates undergo their first appraisal, when their performance is assessed.

Further training is then carried out to keep magistrates up to date with any changes in law and procedure. If magistrates wish to take on more responsibilities or to sit in the Youth Court or the Family Court, they must complete further training.

5 Termination of appointment

5.1 Resignation

Magistrates can resign at any time.

5.2 Retirement

The retirement age for magistrates is 70.

5.3 Removal

Powers to remove a magistrate come from the **Criminal Justice Act 2003**. The Minister for Constitutional Affairs can remove a magistrate for misbehaviour, incompetence, neglect of responsibilities or incapacity.

6 Evaluation

6.1 Advantages

- Members of the community are involved in the criminal justice system.
- Magistrates provide a wide cross-section of views and experience.
- The system is cheap as magistrates are unpaid.
- They receive training so are not complete amateurs.
- The clerk is available to assist them with legal matters.
- Cases can be dealt with more quickly than at the Crown Court.
- They build up skills and knowledge through regular participation.
- They relieve the pressure from other courts.

6.2 Disadvantages

- Magistrates are often criticised as being 'middle-class, middle-aged and middle-minded'.
- They are unrepresentative of local communities in terms of age and ethnic background.
- They do not receive sufficient training.
- The workload is too great.
- They produce inconsistencies in sentencing.
- They rely too much on their legal advisors.
- They are too ready to accept evidence from the prosecution and police.
- They become case-hardened through regular participation.

Consider whether magistrates should be replaced with full-time judges, as this is a regular theme in exam questions.

B Juries

Every year about 450,000 people, selected at random from the electoral roll, undertake jury service. A computer selects those on the roll who are aged between 18 and 70. Due to its random nature some people never get called, while others can be selected more than once. A person has about a one in six chance of being summoned for jury service in his or her lifetime.

1 Selection

Those selected receive a jury summons through the post, advising them that they have been chosen and informing them where they must go and when. They must reply to the jury summons within 7 days. Failure to complete jury service when

summoned is a criminal offence and can be punished with a fine of up to £1,000. Jurors are usually expected to sit for 10 working days and since the average trial lasts about a day and a half, it is highly likely that a juror will sit on more than one trial. Sometimes a juror will be required to sit for more than 10 working days if the trial is expected to last longer.

1.1 Deferral and excusal

Jury service can, however, be deferred under certain circumstances, such as a hospital appointment or a family wedding. If deferred, the person must undertake jury service within 12 months of the original summons. He or she must state which days during the next year that he or she will be available as by law, deferral can only be granted once. Decisions on whether someone may defer or be excused from jury service are made by the Jury Central Summoning Bureau.

Some people, such as members of the armed forces and the medical profession, are often excused and not required to complete jury service. Those who are mentally ill are ineligible for jury service. People with certain criminal convictions are ineligible for jury service. This includes those who have served, or are serving, prison sentences or community orders of varying degrees of seriousness and those on bail in criminal proceedings.

1.2 At court

When a jury is required, a court official chooses a number of jurors (usually 15) at random from those called for duty. Although only 12 are needed for the trial itself, more people are taken into the court in case a juror is unable to sit, for example if they know the defendant or anyone involved in the case.

2 *Role*

Jurors are lay people and as such do not require any legal knowledge. The judges assist them with any points of law and the lawyers aim to make their case as clear as possible so that the jury can understand. Juries are used mainly in criminal trials but occasionally they are also used in civil matters.

2.1 Criminal cases

Juries are only used in about 1% of criminal cases because magistrates deal with the majority of criminal offences. The use of juries is reserved for the more serious cases such as murder, rape and GBH. Trials take place in the Crown Court, with a jury of 12. Since most jurors do not have legal experience, the judge guides them on the relevant law. The role of the jury is to decide on the facts by consideration of the evidence. Jurors then reach a verdict of 'guilty' or 'not guilty'. The jurors must aim to reach a unanimous verdict initially but under the **Juries Act 1974**, majority verdicts (where at least 10 of the jurors agree) are accepted. If the jury has fallen to 10, for example due to illness, then nine must agree. If the defendant is found guilty, the judge passes sentence.

Majority verdicts were introduced to prevent jury tampering.

Juries are often criticised in libel cases for the high level of damages that they award.

2.2 Civil cases

Rarely, jurors may be asked to sit on a civil matter in cases of defamation, fraud, false imprisonment or malicious prosecution. In libel cases, juries decide whether

the defendant is liable or not and if so, how much compensation should be awarded. Such trials are in the High Court or County Court. Additionally, jurors may be required to sit in a coroner's court.

3 Evaluation of juries

3.1 Advantages

- The public participates in the justice system.
- Jury equity, whereby juries make decisions according to their conscience rather than the strict letter of the law.
- Juries are representative of society.
- As they are unpaid, the system is cheap.
- Their deliberations are kept secret and their decisions are made away from external influence.

3.2 Disadvantages

- Juries may not understand the law and reach the wrong decision.
- The secrecy of the jury room means that it is impossible to tell how jurors reached their verdict.
- They do not have to give reasons for their decision so it is difficult to appeal against their verdict.
- They do not receive any training so most are complete amateurs.
- They are more expensive than trial by judge or magistrates alone.
- They may be biased or influenced by the media.

4 Alternatives to juries

Consider the pros and cons of each alternative so that you could produce a balanced argument.

Many suggestions have been made over the years as to how the jury system should be reformed. It should be remembered, however, that juries only deal with 1% of cases. Suggestions are as follows:

- Make juries undergo training prior to sitting on a case.
- Use fewer jurors as there is no good reason why 12 are required.
- Make juries give reasons for their verdicts.
- Allow judges to retire with juries to assist them.
- End trial by jury and replace it with a single judge or panel of judges.
- Have professional jurors.

Summary of Topic 14

Magistrates

1 **Eligibility:** aged 18–65, candidates need not be British nationals but must swear allegiance to the Queen. Candidates must demonstrate that they have the requisite personal qualities, and especially the six key characteristics of good character. Potential magistrates must also be in good health and ensure that they can carry out the necessary duties. Some jobs are regarded as incompatible with the role of a magistrate, e.g. police, traffic wardens and prison workers. An undischarged bankrupt cannot be a magistrate and people with criminal convictions may not be allowed.

2 **Role**

Criminal matters: over 95% of all criminal cases are dealt with by magistrates. They have jurisdiction in both the adult and the youth court. The youth court deals with offenders between the ages of 10 and 17. Magistrates decide on applications for bail and decide the facts and law in trials. If they find a defendant guilty, or the defendant pleads guilty, they must pass an appropriate sentence. This can range from an absolute discharge to 12 months in prison for a single offence. Magistrates may also send certain defendants to the Crown Court for sentencing.

Civil matters: magistrates also have a civil jurisdiction. They deal with those who have not paid their council tax or other fines. Additionally, some magistrates undergo further training in family matters. They can then deal with residence and contact orders regarding children.

3 **Appointment process:** candidates must visit a Magistrates' Court, fill in the application form, be interviewed by the Local Advisory Committee and have a background check. Candidates are recommended to the secretary of state and Lord Chancellor for appointment by Local Advisory Committees.

4 **Training:** once appointed, magistrates must undergo initial training. This lasts about 3 days and may be held over a weekend. The new magistrate must make at least three court observations and visit a prison and a young offenders' institute. All new magistrates are given a mentor to assist them. The mentor will be an experienced magistrate from the local area whose role is to offer guidance and support.

5 **Termination of appointment:** magistrates can resign, retire at 70 years old or be removed for misbehaviour, incompetence, neglect of responsibilities or incapacity.

6 **Evaluation**

Advantages include: involvement of the community; cross-section of society; cheap; have some training; have a legal advisor; quicker than a Crown Court trial.

Disadvantages include: 'middle-class, middle-aged and middle-minded'; do not receive sufficient training; produce inconsistencies in sentencing; are too ready to accept evidence from the prosecution and police.

Juries

1 **Selection:** a computer randomly selects those on the electoral roll who are aged between 18 and 70. Due to its random nature, some people never get called while others can be selected more than once. A person has about a one in six chance of being summoned for jury service in his or her lifetime. Jury service can, however, be deferred under certain circumstances, such as a hospital appointment or a family wedding. Some people, such as members of the armed forces, are excused from jury service. Those who are mentally ill are ineligible for jury service. People with certain criminal convictions are ineligible for jury service. This includes those who have served, or are serving, prison sentences or community orders of varying degrees of seriousness and those on bail in criminal proceedings.

2 **Role**

Criminal cases: juries are only used in about 1% of criminal cases because magistrates deal with the majority of criminal offences. The use of juries is

reserved for the more serious cases such as murder, rape and GBH. Trials take place in the Crown Court, with a jury of 12. Since most jurors do not have legal experience, the judge guides them on the relevant law. The role of the jury is to decide on the facts by consideration of the evidence. Jurors then reach a verdict of 'guilty' or 'not guilty'.

Civil cases: rarely, jurors may be asked to sit on a civil matter in cases of defamation, fraud, false imprisonment or malicious prosecution. In libel cases juries decide whether the defendant is liable or not and if so, how much compensation should be awarded. Such trials are held in the High Court or County Court. Additionally, jurors may be required to sit in a coroner's court.

3 **Evaluation**

Advantages include: the public participates in the justice system; juries are representative of society; cheap; their deliberations are kept secret and their decisions are made away from external influence.

Disadvantages include: juries may not understand the law; they do not receive any training; they may be biased or influenced by the media.

4 **Alternatives to juries:** many suggestions have been made over the years as to how the jury system should be reformed, e.g. professional jurors; training for jurors; allow judges to retire with juries to assist them; or end trial by jury and replace juries with a single judge or panel of judges.

One of the major concerns for anyone involved in a court case is the cost involved. Lawyers and courts are notoriously expensive. In civil matters, this may simply mean that many people decide not to proceed with their case and thus are denied access to justice. In criminal cases, the effect could be that those unable to meet the costs of their defence are unable to obtain advice, assistance and representation and thus are denied a fair trial. To avoid this, public funding or 'legal aid' is available in some instances to cover both civil and criminal cases.

A Legal Services Commission

The Legal Services Commission (LSC) administers legal aid in England and Wales. It was established under the **Access to Justice Act 1999** and replaced the old Legal Aid Board. The Department for Constitutional Affairs is responsible for the LSC and is accountable to Parliament for its performance. The LSC has 15 offices in England and Wales and employs about 1,800 staff, who help about 2 million people a year.

The LSC administers two different schemes, depending upon whether it is a civil or a criminal matter. The Community Legal Service deals with civil legal aid, while criminal legal aid is administered by the Criminal Defence Service. The LSC's total annual budget is around £2 billion.

B Community Legal Service

The Community Legal Service (CLS) administers civil advice and assistance at a cost of £846 million in 2004/05. Contracts are negotiated with firms of solicitors with the relevant expertise, and the firms are then paid on a monthly basis. Only those firms of solicitors with a contract can carry out publicly funded work. To get a contract, the solicitors' firm needs to have a 'Quality Mark', which is only awarded after inspection by the CLS.

The 'Quality Mark' can also be awarded to other advice providers, such as citizens' advice bureaux, law centres and community organisations. This ensures that needs are met throughout England and Wales and people can access whatever information, advice and assistance they require. The most common matters that people seek assistance for are debt, asylum, housing, employment, community care and education.

The assistance received differs according to the type of problem, but ranges from advice to taking cases to court.

1 Services

You must be able to describe the different types of help available.

The Community Legal Service provides a number of different types of help in civil matters.

1.1 Legal advice

This provides those who are eligible (see below) with up to 2 hours of advice and assistance with any legal problem.

1.2 Help at court

An eligible party is allowed to have a solicitor or advisor to speak for him or her at a court hearing.

1.3 Approved family help

In family cases, help is available to assist in resolving disputes, often using mediation. Mediation is a type of dispute resolution that helps parties to reach an agreement.

1.4 Legal representation

Legal representation is available in court for both claimants and defendants. Two types of assistance are available: investigative help allows the strength of a claim to be assessed; full representation covers legal representation in court proceedings.

2 Eligibility

To qualify for some types of civil legal aid, certain conditions must be met and the applicant must not exceed certain financial limits.

2.1 Legal help, help at court and legal representation

Assistance is only given if there is a benefit to the client and it is reasonable for the matter to be funded. The applicant's monthly income must not exceed £2,288. If his or her income is less than £2,288 the applicant must have a disposable income of less than £632, i.e. after tax, national insurance and an allowance for any dependants have been deducted. A partner's income can also be taken into account. For the Legal Representation Scheme, a contribution has to be made by anyone with a disposable income of between £232 and the £632 limit. Additionally, any capital, e.g. savings, stocks and bonds, must be under £8,000. A contribution may be required from those with between £3,000 and £8,000. Those in receipt of income-based Job Seeker's Allowance automatically qualify.

3 Conditional fee agreements

Following the **Access to Justice Act 1999**, some cases that previously qualified for legal aid were no longer eligible for public funding. Personal injury cases fell into this category and those who wished to make such a claim had to find alternative means of funding it. Potential claimants with enough money could fund the cases themselves but this was prohibitively expensive for many who sought an alternative. To meet this need, conditional fee agreements (CFAs) were heavily promoted by solicitors and personal injury firms.

Often advertised under the slogan 'No win, no fee', CFAs were introduced by the **Courts and Legal Services Act 1990**. A written agreement is made between a solicitor and a client and usually it is agreed that the client will not have to pay the solicitor's costs if he or she loses the case. However, the client may still have to pay the costs of the other side and other expenses relating to the case and he or she should be advised to take out insurance to cover these. If the client wins, he or she pays the solicitor's fee plus an added percentage — sometimes known as an 'uplift fee'. This is to compensate the solicitor for taking the risk of non-payment. Usually, the higher the risk of losing, the higher the uplift fee but such fees are capped at twice the usual fee. Since the **Access to Justice Act 1999**, solicitors' costs, including the uplift fee, are recoverable from the losing party.

The obvious advantages of CFAs are that they remove the expense of these cases from public funds, leaving more money for other types of cases. They provide a way of proceeding with a case that most clients could not otherwise afford. There has been some criticism of CFAs, however. Insurance to cover the costs of the other side can be prohibitively expensive but without it, the client may face an enormous bill if he or she loses, since the losing party usually has to pay the costs of the winning party. Critics have suggested that since solicitors will seek to minimise the chances of not being paid, they will only accept strong cases that they are confident they can win. This leaves those with weaker, borderline cases with a much lower chance of being able to proceed with their claim unless they can fund it themselves.

> Ensure that you can argue for and against these types of arrangements.

C Criminal Defence Service

The Legal Services Commission is also responsible for public funding in criminal cases and the majority of its budget is spent here. As in civil funding, the LSC has set up an organisation to administer criminal legal aid, known as the Criminal Defence Service (CDS). Solicitors and others who wish to carry out work funded by the CDS must apply for a contract and are regularly checked to make sure that they are providing high-quality work at a reasonable cost. Criminal legal aid covers those suspected or accused of a criminal offence and enables them to access such advice and representation as required. The aim is to ensure that such people receive a fair hearing and are able to respond properly to the allegations against them. It is a requirement of the **Human Rights Act 1998** that people receive a fair trial, and not being able to afford legal assistance would obviously jeopardise this.

1 Types of help

1.1 Advice and assistance

> As with civil legal aid, you must be able to describe the various types of assistance available.

This service funds help from a solicitor, including giving general advice, writing letters, negotiating, and getting a barrister's opinion. There is a means test and a client is not eligible if his or her disposable income exceeds £1,000 a month.

1.2 Police station advice and assistance

Anyone questioned over an offence — whether arrested or not — can get free legal advice from a contracted solicitor. This type of help is not means tested. The person involved can choose between the duty solicitor, another solicitor from a police list or his or her own solicitor, if he or she has one.

1.3 Advocacy assistance

This provides the cost of a solicitor preparing a case and initial representation in certain proceedings in the Magistrates' and Crown Courts. It also covers representation for defendants who have not paid a civil fine or those who have breached a civil court order and are at risk of imprisonment. Such assistance is subject to a merits test but there is no means test. The merits test considers, among other things, the chances of the defendant losing his or her liberty or reputation, whether expert cross-examination is needed and if the defendant will be able to understand the proceedings.

1.4 Representation in court

Those charged with or summoned for a criminal offence can apply for funding to cover the cost of a solicitor to prepare a defence and for representation in court. If a barrister is needed, these costs will also be met. If necessary, advice regarding an appeal is also covered.

1.5 Duty solicitors

These solicitors are available either at the police station or at the Magistrates' Court and give free legal advice to those who require their assistance.

Summary of Topic 15

Legal Services Commission

The Legal Services Commission (LSC) administers legal aid in England and Wales. It was established under the **Access to Justice Act 1999** and replaced the old Legal Aid Board. The Department for Constitutional Affairs is responsible for the LSC and is accountable to Parliament for its performance.

Community Legal Service

The Community Legal Service (CLS) administers civil advice and assistance. The assistance received differs according to the type of problem. It includes legal advice, help at court, approved family help and legal representation. Conditional fee agreements are now used for personal injury cases.

Criminal Defence Service

The Legal Services Commission is also responsible for public funding in criminal cases and the majority of its budget is spent here. Types of help include: advice and assistance, police station advice and assistance, advocacy assistance, representation in court and duty solicitors.

Most crimes require the perpetrator to commit the '*actus reus*' (guilty act) while having the required '*mens rea*' (guilty mind). This is designed to ensure that only those deemed blameworthy are convicted and punished. The *actus reus* and *mens rea* of a crime differs according to the nature of the offence, but the prosecution must prove both beyond reasonable doubt to secure a guilty verdict.

A *Actus reus*

You must learn the different types of *actus reus* and be able to give an example of each.

Actus reus is Latin for 'guilty act' but this is a simplistic definition. The *actus reus* is made up of all of the parts of the crime except the defendant's mental state. There are several different types of *actus reus*.

1 Conduct crimes

Here the *actus reus* is simply prohibited conduct. Perjury is an example of a conduct crime, where the defendant is guilty if he or she lies under oath in court. Even if the court does not believe the defendant's lie, the conduct will still be a criminal offence.

2 State of affairs crimes

For these offences the *actus reus* involves 'being' rather than 'doing' — it is the circumstances that exist that make it an offence. Thus the prosecution need only prove the existence of those circumstances. Rape is an example as it is not the sexual act itself that makes it a crime, but rather the surrounding circumstances, i.e. that it was carried out without consent.

Remember to include cases to improve your marks.

R v *Larsonneur* (1933)
The defendant was a French woman who was deported from Ireland and forcibly taken to the UK. When she arrived in England she was promptly arrested for being an illegal alien, contrary to the Aliens Order 1920. She had been found in the UK when she did not have permission to be there. She was convicted and appealed on the basis that immigration officers had taken her to the UK against her will but the Court of Appeal upheld her conviction.

Winzar v *Chief Constable of Kent* (1983)
The defendant was convicted of being found drunk on a highway in contravention of the **Licensing Act 1872**. He appealed on the basis that he had been taken onto the road by the police, who had removed him from a hospital when there were complaints about his drunken behaviour. His conviction was upheld — he was drunk on a highway despite the fact that he had been taken there involuntarily.

3 Result crimes

The prosecution must prove that the defendant's actions caused the prohibited result — for example murder, where the prosecution must prove that it was the defendant's actions that caused the death of the victim. In order to establish this, the prosecution must prove a causal link between the action and the consequence.

3.1 Factual causation

First, the prosecution must prove factual causation: as a matter of fact, did the defendant's actions cause the harm? The test for factual causation is the 'but for' test — but for the defendant's actions, would the victim have suffered harm? If not, then the test is satisfied.

> **R v White (1910)**
>
> The defendant decided to kill his mother in order to gain his inheritance. He put poison in her drink but before she consumed enough to kill her she died of a heart attack. The prosecution could not prove that the defendant's actions were the factual cause of her death: 'but for' his actions she would still have died. The defendant was, however, liable for attempted murder.

3.2 Legal causation

Once the prosecution has proved factual causation, it must then prove legal causation. The test for this is whether the defendant's conduct made a 'significant contribution' to the result. The defendant's actions do not need to be the only or even the main cause of the harm.

This is sometimes known as the *'de minimis'* rule, whereby the defendant's actions were more than a minimal cause of the result.

Sometimes there may be more than one factor contributing to the final result. This is described as a 'chain of causation'. For the defendant to be guilty, there must be an unbroken chain of causation directly from his or her actions to the end result. The chain of causation may be affected by a number of things.

3.2a Actions of the victim

The actions of the victim may break the chain of causation, but only if they are unreasonable.

> **R v Roberts (1978)**
>
> The defendant was giving a lift to the victim and began touching her clothes. The victim jumped from the moving car to escape as she thought that the defendant was going to rape her. The defendant was held liable for her injuries as they were a reasonably foreseeable result of his actions. Only if the victim does something so 'daft' that it cannot be expected will the chain of causation be broken.

3.2b Actions of a third party

The actions of a third party may break the chain of causation but, as with actions of the victim, they will not if they are reasonably foreseeable.

R v *Pagett* (1983)

The defendant was being chased by armed police and in order to try to escape he took his girlfriend hostage. He then fired at the police, using her as a human shield. The police returned fire and the girl was killed. Pagett tried to argue that he was not the cause of her death but the court held that it was reasonably foreseeable that the police would return fire if shot at and his conviction was upheld.

If the victim has received negligent medical treatment, this will not break the chain of causation unless it is 'palpably wrong' — as in *R v Jordan* (1956).

R v *Jordan* (1956)

The defendant had stabbed the victim who had been recovering well until being given a large quantity of drugs that he was allergic to, and he died. The treatment was described as 'palpably wrong' and the Court of Appeal said that as such it broke the chain of causation. This meant that Jordan was not responsible for the defendant's murder. Since then, a number of cases have referred to *Jordan* as being dependent upon its exact facts, and it is unlikely to be followed. Indeed, it is rare that medical treatment would break the chain of causation, since the courts take the view that it would not have been required were it not for the conduct of the defendant.

R v *Smith* (1959)

The defendant and the victim were both soldiers. The victim was stabbed and was then dropped twice while being taken to the medical officer, who failed to appreciate the severity of his injuries. After a delay, treatment was administered but it did not help and indeed may have made the situation worse. The victim died of the stab wound and the Court of Appeal upheld the defendant's conviction, despite the negligent treatment. At the time of the victim's death the stab wound was still an operating and substantial cause.

R v *Cheshire* (1991)

The defendant shot the victim after a fight in a fish and chip shop. In hospital the victim received negligent treatment and eventually died after developing a respiratory infection causing breathing difficulties. The defendant's conviction for murder was upheld despite the fact that the original wounds were no longer life-threatening when the victim died. The Court of Appeal held that, even if the negligent treatment was the immediate cause of death, it still would not break the chain of causation unless it was so independent of the defendant's actions that it rendered them insignificant.

Switching off a life-support machine does not break the chain of causation.

R v *Malcherek*, R v *Steel* (1981)

In *Malcherek* the defendant stabbed his wife, who suffered irreparable brain damage from a blood clot. Doctors carried out the relevant tests and then switched off her life-support machine when it was determined that she suffered brain death. In *Steel* the defendant had attacked the victim, causing severe head injuries. She never regained consciousness and her life-support

machine was switched off. Both men were convicted of murder and appealed on the basis that the cause of death was the switching off of the life-support machine. As doctors will not switch off machines until tests have established brain-stem death, the Court of Appeal upheld both murder convictions.

3.2c The thin skull test

If some infirmity of the victim has made the result more severe than it would ordinarily be, the defendant cannot argue that the chain of causation has been broken.

This rule is sometimes referred to as 'you take your victims as you find them'.

R v *Blaue* (1975)

The defendant stabbed his victim after she refused to have sex with him. In hospital the victim refused a blood transfusion on the grounds that as she was a Jehovah's Witness it was against her religious beliefs to undergo the procedure. Medical opinion was that she would not have died if she had had the transfusion. The defendant's conviction for manslaughter was upheld despite his argument that the victim's refusal to accept treatment was unreasonable and should therefore break the chain of causation. The court took the view that the defendant had to take his victim as he found her, including any religious beliefs that she may hold.

Make a case list to help with your revision. Write down the name of the case, brief facts and the point that it is used to illustrate.

B Voluntary conduct

The general rule is that in order to be liable, the defendant's conduct must be voluntary. So, for example, a person hitting out due to a reflex action would not be liable as the courts would be unlikely to find that his or her actions were undertaken voluntarily.

Leicester v *Pearson* (1952)

A driver did not stop for a pedestrian on a zebra crossing but his actions were held to be involuntary as another driver had driven into him from behind and pushed him forward onto the crossing.

As can be seen by the cases of *Larsonneur* and *Winzar*, however, sometimes the courts do not interpret the term 'voluntary' in the way that most people would (see page 108).

C Omissions

An omission is simply a failure to do something. The general rule in criminal law is that a person is not usually liable for his or her omissions. Examples are often given of a stranger who sees an unknown child drowning in a river and fails to assist, even though he could easily save the child. In this case there would be no prosecution as the defendant had no duty under UK law to act — there is no

Learn each situation in which a person may be liable for an omission and the corresponding case.

requirement that people help each other. Occasionally, however, the courts may find that a defendant is liable for his or her failure to act. In certain circumstances the court may find that a person was under a duty to act — for example if the stranger in the example above had pushed the child into the river or if the child belonged to the defendant. In those cases the defendant would probably face prosecution if he or she failed to assist. There are different circumstances that give rise to a duty to act.

1 Special relationship

A clear example of a relationship that gives rise to a duty to act is that of parents and children. Parents owe a duty to look after their children and may be prosecuted if they fail to do so. Biological parents are obviously included but the courts can impose a duty even if there is no blood relation between the parties involved.

> **R v *Gibbins and Proctor* (1918)**
> A father and his girlfriend were living together with the man's daughter. They failed to feed the child and the Court of Appeal upheld their conviction for murder when she starved to death.

2 Contractual duty

If a defendant is under a contractual duty to act and fails to do so, he or she may be liable if others are likely to be injured as a result.

> **R v *Pittwood* (1902)**
> The defendant was a gatekeeper at a level crossing. One day he left the gate open and went for lunch. A hay cart attempting to cross the line was hit by a train. The defendant was convicted of manslaughter when the driver died. His conviction was based on his failure to perform his contractual duty — to shut the gate when the train was approaching.

3 Professional duty

> **R v *Dytham* (1979)**
> A police officer who watched a man being kicked to death but failed to intervene or summon assistance was guilty of misconduct in a public office as he had neglected to protect the victim or apprehend his attackers.

4 Voluntary acceptance of responsibility for another

A duty to act may also be imposed where someone voluntarily accepts responsibility for another.

> **R v *Stone and Dobinson* (1977)**
> The defendants, common-law husband and wife, were of low intelligence. After a visit from Stone's anorexic sister, Fanny, they decided to take her in

and look after her. Over the following weeks Fanny became increasingly ill. She became confined to bed and eventually died of blood poisoning as a result of infected bedsores. The defendants were convicted of manslaughter and their convictions were upheld on appeal. They had voluntarily assumed a duty to look after Fanny, knowing that she was relying on them, and their failure to summon medical assistance had contributed to her death.

5 Creating a dangerous situation

If someone creates a risk to another's life or property, he or she is under a duty to act in order to stop or at least limit the harm caused. If he or she does not do so, he or she may be liable for any resulting consequences.

R v Miller (1983)

The defendant was a squatter in a house and one night he fell asleep on a mattress while smoking a cigarette. When he was woken by the flames he got up, moved to another room and went back to sleep, doing nothing to stop the spread of the fire. The fire caused significant damage to the house and the defendant was convicted of criminal damage. The House of Lords upheld his conviction and said that on realising that he had created the dangerous situation, the defendant had a responsibility to limit the harmful effects of the fire. He could easily have done this by calling the fire brigade and his failure to do so left him liable for the damage.

D *Mens rea*

Mens rea is Latin for 'guilty mind' and concerns the mind-set of the defendant when the *actus reus* was committed. Along with the *actus reus*, it is a necessary requirement of most criminal offences — except those classed as strict liability (see pages 118–20). *Mens rea* generally allows the blameworthy to be punished, not least by distinguishing between those who commit the *actus reus* of an offence accidentally and those who take an unjustifiable risk of harm or who deliberately set out to commit a crime.

There are several types of *mens rea* and different crimes have different *mens rea* requirements. To be liable for theft, for example, the defendant must have acted dishonestly with the intention of permanently depriving the owner of his or her property. For murder, the defendant must have intended to kill or cause really serious harm.

Two of the most commonly required types of *mens rea* are intention and recklessness.

1 Intention

Many crimes require that the defendant had the necessary intent when committing the offence. It is a subjective test that requires the court to establish what the defendant him- or herself was thinking.

Intention is a word in common use but it has two distinct meanings in the context of *mens rea*, direct intent and indirect oblique intent.

1.1 Direct intent

In its simplest form, direct intent means that the defendant set out to achieve a particular result or consequence. It is sometimes explained by saying that the defendant foresaw a particular result as a certainty and wanted to bring it about. It was defined in *Moloney* (see below) as 'a true desire to bring about the consequences'. An example would be where the defendant shoots a victim in the chest because the defendant wants to kill him or her.

1.2 Indirect/oblique intent

Many crimes require the prosecution to prove that when committing the *actus reus* the defendant was acting either intentionally or recklessly (see below). For some crimes, however, the prosecution will not be able to rely on recklessness but will need to prove beyond reasonable doubt that the defendant intended to bring about the consequences.

These are known as 'specific intent' crimes.

Sometimes a defendant will claim that he or she did not intend the result and indeed did not want it to occur. If this is so, then the defendant is not guilty and must be acquitted. The problem occurs, however, when the result was virtually certain to occur but the defendant is denying that he or she intended it, saying that it was not his or her aim to bring it about. An example might be where a terrorist blows up a plane to kill one of the passengers. The terrorist may claim that he or she did not want to kill any passengers other than the intended target, but by blowing up a plane all passengers are virtually certain to be killed. The defendant could therefore be said to have intended their deaths if he or she knew that they were virtually certain to occur and despite recognising this, he or she was determined to continue. Not surprisingly, this issue has posed many problems, and a number of cases have come before the courts to determine the meaning of indirect or oblique intent.

R v Moloney (1985)

The defendant was a soldier and after a family party, he and his stepfather had a race to see who could load and fire a gun in the fastest time. Moloney was quicker and pointed the gun at his stepfather, who challenged him to fire it. Moloney promptly did so, hitting his stepfather in the head and killing him. At trial, Moloney claimed that he never intended to kill the victim or even to cause him serious harm, and that he was just joking around. The House of Lords substituted his murder conviction for one of manslaughter, stating that only an intention to kill or to cause serious injury was sufficient for murder. The House of Lords said the jury should ask if death or serious injury was a natural consequence of the defendant's actions. If so, they should then go on to consider whether the defendant himself realised this. If so, this was evidence from which they could infer that the defendant did have the required intent.

R v *Hancock and Shankland* (1986)

During the miner's strike the defendants pushed concrete blocks off a motorway bridge. They were trying to block the road so that a taxi taking another miner to work would not be able to get past. One of the blocks hit the windscreen of the taxi and the driver was killed. The defendants claimed that their intention was to block the road rather than to kill the driver. The House of Lords substituted their murder convictions for those of manslaughter. They emphasised that the probability or chance of the consequence occurring must be taken into account. The more probable the result was, the more likely that the defendant foresaw it, and the more likely that he foresaw it, the more likely he could be said to have intended it.

R v *Nedrick* (1986)

The defendant held a grudge against a woman and intended to frighten her by pushing a lighted substance through her letterbox. Fire broke out in the house and the woman's child was killed. After a misdirection by the trial judge, the Court of Appeal said that the jury should determine whether the defendant had the required intention by asking two questions. First, how probable the consequence was and second, whether the defendant foresaw it. If death or serious bodily harm was virtually certain to occur and the defendant appreciated this, then the jury could use this as evidence that he had the necessary intention.

R v *Woollin* (1998)

The defendant lost his temper when his 3-month-old son started choking on his food and picked him up, shook him and then threw him across the room towards his pram. The baby died as a result of his injuries. At trial, the defendant claimed that he had not intended to kill his son and had not wanted him to die. The judge told the jury that they could convict if they were satisfied that the defendant had seen a 'substantial risk' of serious injury. On appeal, the House of Lords confirmed that the consequence must be a virtually certain result of the defendant's actions and the defendant must appreciate this.

> This is difficult to understand at first, so you may need to read through it several times.

In conclusion, direct intent is where the defendant actually wanted the result and indirect/oblique intent is where the defendant did not necessarily want the result but foresaw it to a point of virtual certainty and was determined to carry on anyway.

2 Recklessness

Another commonly required type of *mens rea* is recklessness, which covers the situation when a defendant takes an unjustifiable risk. As with intention, it is a subjective test and the defendant must recognise the risk that he or she is running. Recklessness was defined in the case of *R* v *Cunningham* (1957).

B   Battery

Section 39 **Criminal Justice Act 1988** provides that battery is a summary offence, punishable by up to 6 months' imprisonment or a fine. This offence is also a common-law offence.

1   *Actus reus*

The *actus reus* of battery consists of the application of unlawful force on another. Any unlawful physical contact can amount to a battery; there is no need to prove harm or pain, and a mere touch can be sufficient.

A battery can be direct or indirect. Direct is force applied directly by one person to another, e.g. a slap or a punch. Indirect force can be applied using an implement or vehicle.

> *These cases are examples of indirect battery.*

Fagan v Metropolitan Police Commissioner (1969)
The defendant drove onto the foot of a police officer and was guilty of battery.

Haystead v DPP (2000)
The defendant punched a woman who was holding a baby. She dropped the baby. The defendant was found guilty of a battery against the baby, as he had indirectly applied force.

To constitute a battery, the victim need not be aware that he or she is about to be struck. Therefore if someone is struck from behind, this will still constitute a battery; the victim need not see it coming.

Force does not have to be applied to the person's body. Touching his or her clothing may be enough, even if the victim feels nothing at all as a result.

R v Thomas (1985)
The judge stated that touching a woman's skirt was equivalent to touching the woman herself.

2   *Mens rea*

The *mens rea* of battery is intention or Cunningham recklessness, i.e. intention or recklessness as to application of unlawful force.

Often, the offences of assault and battery occur at the same time. This is known as common assault.

C   Actual bodily harm (s.47)

> *Actual bodily harm and grievous bodily harm are defined in the **Offences Against the Person Act 1861**.*

Section 47 **Offences Against the Person Act 1861** states that it is an offence to commit 'any assault occasioning actual bodily harm'. The offence is triable either way and carries a maximum sentence of 5 years' imprisonment.

1 ## Actus reus

The *actus reus* of actual bodily harm (ABH) has been interpreted as being committed with either assault or battery. Therefore to prove the *actus reus* of ABH is the same as to prove the *actus reus* for assault/battery. In addition, the prosecution must prove that the assault/battery caused (occasioned) ABH.

ABH is defined in *R v Chan-Fook* (1994).

ABH has been given a wide definition. In *R v Miller* (1954) the court stated: 'Actual bodily harm includes hurt or injury calculated to interfere with health or comfort.' Thus ABH can occur where discomfort to the person is caused. However, in *R v Chan-Fook* (1994) Lord Justice Hobhouse said in the Court of Appeal: 'The word "actual" indicates that the injury (although there is no need for it to be permanent) should not be so trivial as to be wholly insignificant.'

ABH can include psychiatric injury/nervous shock, but not mere emotions such as fear/distress or panic. The injury must be an identifiable clinical condition (*R v Ireland*, 1997 and *R v Burstow*, 1997).

2 ## Mens rea

The *mens rea* for ABH is the same as for assault and battery. No additional *mens rea* is required.

R v Roberts (1978)
Late at night the defendant gave a lift in his car to a girl. During the journey he began to make sexual advances, touching the girl's clothes. Frightened that he was going to rape her, she jumped out of the moving car, injuring herself. It was held that the defendant had committed the *actus reus* of a s.47 offence by touching the girl's clothing, i.e. a battery, and this act had caused her to suffer ABH. The defendant argued that he neither intended to cause her ABH nor had he seen any risk of her suffering ABH as a result of his advances. This argument was rejected; the court held that the *mens rea* for battery was sufficient in itself and there was no need for any extra *mens rea* regarding ABH.

The decision in *R v Roberts* (1978) was confirmed in *R v Savage* (1991).

R v Savage (1991)
The defendant went to a local pub, where she spotted her husband's new girlfriend having a drink with some friends. She went up to the table intending to throw a pint of beer over the girlfriend. On reaching the table she said 'Nice to meet you darling' and threw the beer, but as she did so she accidentally let go of the glass as well, which broke and cut the woman's wrist. The defendant argued that she lacked sufficient *mens rea* to be liable for a s.47 offence because her intention had only been to throw the beer and she had not seen the risk that the glass might injure the woman. This was rejected because she intended to apply unlawful force (the *mens rea* for battery) and there was no need to prove that she intended or was reckless as to causing ABH.

D Grievous bodily harm (s.20)

The difference between s.20 and s.47 is one of degree; GBH is much more serious.

Section 20 **Offences Against the Person Act 1861** states: 'Whosoever shall unlawfully and maliciously wound or inflict any grievous bodily harm upon any other person either with or without any weapon or instrument shall be guilty of an offence triable either way and being convicted thereof shall be liable to imprisonment for 5 years.'

1 *Actus reus*

Grievous bodily harm is defined in *R* v *Smith* (1959).

The *actus reus* of grievous bodily harm (GBH) is inflicting any GBH. In *DPP* v *Smith* (1961) the House of Lords emphasised that GBH should be given its ordinary meaning, i.e. 'really serious harm'. This was confirmed in *R* v *Saunders* (1985), where the Court of Appeal said there is no real difference in meaning between 'serious' and 'really serious'.

The word 'inflict' has been interpreted to mean that the GBH must be caused by the direct application of force, e.g. hitting, kicking or stabbing, but not by for example digging a hole for someone to fall into. In practice, however, the courts have given a fairly wide interpretation as to when force is direct.

> ### *R* v *Martin* (1881)
> While a play was being performed at a theatre the defendant placed an iron bar across the exit, turned off the staircase lights and shouted 'fire'. The audience panicked and in the rush to escape people were seriously injured. The defendant was found liable under s.20, even though, strictly speaking, on these facts it is difficult to view the application of force as truly direct.

> ### *R* v *Halliday* (1896)
> This is another wide interpretation of the word 'inflict'. The defendant's behaviour frightened his wife so much that she jumped out of their bedroom window to get away from him. The injuries that she suffered as a result of the fall were found to have been directly applied, so that her husband could be liable under s.20.

A 'wound' requires a break in the first two layers of skin, so there is normally bleeding, although a graze will be sufficient.

> ### *C* v *Eisenhower* (1984)
> The defendant fired an air pistol, hitting the victim in the eye with a pellet. This ruptured a blood vessel in the eye, causing internal bleeding, but this was not sufficient to constitute a 'wounding' as the skin had not been broken.

2 ## Mens rea

The *mens rea* of s.20 GBH is described by the old-fashioned word 'maliciously'. In *R* v *Cunningham* (1957) it was stated that for purposes of the 1861 Act, 'maliciously' meant 'intentionally' or 'recklessly'.

There is no need to intend GBH or wounding, or to be reckless as to whether GBH or wounding might be caused. The defendant need only intend that or be reckless as to whether his or her actions could have caused some physical damage.

R v Grimshaw (1984)

The defendant was in a pub when she heard someone insult her boyfriend. She turned round and struck the person, pushing the glass he was holding in his face and causing considerable injury. She was found guilty under s.20: she had inflicted GBH and she had the *mens rea* because she had at least foreseen that the man would suffer some harm. Therefore, if the defendant realises that some slight injury might be caused as a result of his or her act, that realisation makes him or her guilty under s.20.

R v Parmenter (1991)

The defendant threw a baby into the air and caught it, causing GBH. The defendant said he had done this before with slightly older children and was unaware that his actions were likely to cause harm to a young baby. The judge held that the defendant was not guilty as he did not intend to injure the child, nor did he realise there was a risk of injury to the child.

E # Grievous bodily harm (s.18)

Section 18 **Offences Against the Person Act 1861** states: 'Whosoever shall unlawfully and maliciously by any means whatsoever wound or cause any grievous bodily harm to any person, with intent to do some grievous bodily harm to any person, or with intent to resist or prevent the lawful apprehension or detainer of any person, shall be guilty of an offence triable only on indictment, and being convicted thereof shall be liable to imprisonment for life.'

1 ## Actus reus

This is similar to s.20 and requires proof of either GBH or wounding. The *actus reus* of wounding and GBH have the same meaning as under s.20.

2 ## Mens rea

To satisfy the *mens rea* the prosecution must prove intention, i.e. intention to cause GBH or an intention to avoid arrest. The crucial difference between s.20 and s.18 GBH is in the *mens rea*: while recklessness can be sufficient for s.20, intention is always required for s.18.

Negligence is a type of 'tort'. Tort (the French word for 'wrong') is a word used when referring to civil laws. Civil law differs from criminal law. Civil cases are disputes between individuals. The claimant in a civil case sues the defendant in order to prove that the defendant is liable (usually because the claimant wants compensation). There are many different torts, e.g. nuisance (disputes between neighbours), defamation (claiming that a newspaper printed something untrue) and negligence.

In order to prove negligence, three things must be established: duty of care, breach of duty and damage.

A Duty of care

The neighbour principle, established by Lord Atkin in *Donoghue* v *Stevenson* (1932) House of Lords, was the traditional way in which the court decided if a duty of care was owed. If a person was 'so closely and directly affected by your acts or omission' then you owed a duty of care.

Donoghue v *Stevenson* (1932)
Donoghue suffered gastroenteritis after drinking a bottle of ginger beer that contained a dead snail. She sued Stevenson, the company that manufactured the drink. Donoghue had been bought the drink by a friend and therefore she could not make a claim under contract law. The House of Lords made a landmark decision when it decided that there was a duty of care. Lord Atkin established the 'neighbour principle' so the courts were able to decide who owed a duty of care.

After *Donoghue* v *Stevenson* (1932) established the 'neighbour principle', the courts were able to decide who owed a duty of care. Judges found themselves making policy decisions to avoid certain people owing a duty of care, even when they were closely and directly affected.

> A policy decision is where a judge decides a case according to what is in the interest of the public.

The neighbour principle has since been modified into a three-stage test, which uses an incremental approach. This is where once a duty of care has been established, e.g. doctor/patient, it is not necessary to prove a duty exists in future doctor/patient cases. This approach also means that judges will add new categories of duty of care by analogy, e.g. doctor/patient led to nurse/patient etc. This way a judge will follow the precedent set in an earlier case. For example, *Ross* v *Caunters* (1980) established that a solicitor does owe a duty to his or her clients. Other established categories include doctor and patient, motorist and other road user etc.

> It is not necessary for you to know the facts of *Caparo Industries* v *Dickman* (1990).

In novel situations the judges will decide whether a new category should be added by analogy with the existing ones. This test was defined in *Caparo Industries plc* v *Dickman* (1990).

A *Duty of care*

> **Caparo Industries plc v Dickman (1990)**
> The House of Lords modernised the neighbour principle. The new three-part test became:
> 1 Was the damage reasonably foreseeable?
> 2 Was there sufficient proximity between the claimant and the defendant?
> 3 Is it just and fair to impose a duty of care?
> If the court satisfies all three, a duty of care is established. This case involved investors trying to get compensation for shares they bought which lost money.

1 Was the damage reasonably foreseeable?

An objective test is where the court decides liability based on the ordinary reasonable man rather than the people involved in the case.

Foresight of consequences is necessary. If the 'ordinary reasonable man' could not foresee the damage to the defendant, then a duty of care is not owed.

> **Bourhill v Young (1943)**
> It was not foreseeable that a woman would suffer a miscarriage after hearing a motorbike accident. The defendant did not owe a duty of care to the claimant.

> **Maguire v Harland and Wolff plc (2005)**
> The claimant got ill from asbestos that her husband had on his work clothes. She tried to claim compensation from his employers. This case dates back to 1965, when the dangers of asbestos were not known. It was not foreseeable that she would get ill and therefore her husband's employers did not owe a duty of care.

2 Was there sufficient proximity between the claimant and the defendant?

Proximity is distance in time or space.

Proximity requires that the claimant and defendant have a legal connection. This link can either be a physical connection (*Donoghue* v *Stevenson*, 1932) or a relationship (*McLoughlin* v *O'Brian*, 1983).

> **McLoughlin v O'Brian (1983)**
> The claimant was able to claim compensation for nervous shock from the lorry driver who had caused an accident that had seriously injured her family. There was an obvious proximity between the lorry driver and the claimant's family, but the court held that there was proximity between the lorry driver and the claimant as well. She had not witnessed the accident but she had seen her family at the hospital.

3 Is it just and fair to impose a duty of care?

Judges can misuse this part of the test to make sure that certain people do not owe a duty of care.

> **Griffiths v Lindsay (1998)**
> The court decided that it was not fair for a taxi driver to owe a duty of care to a drunk passenger who got run over as he got out of the taxi.

B Breach of duty

This is the **fault** element of negligence. Just because the defendant is a doctor (duty of care) and one of her patients has died (damage), it does not mean that she has been negligent. She must have committed an act or omission that fell below the **standard of care** expected of her.

The standard of care required is described as a general standard. You do not have to reach the standard of a really good doctor, just an average doctor. Breach of duty is established using the **objective test** (the standard of the ordinary reasonable man, or in this example, ordinary reasonable doctor).

A general standard of care creates consistent application of the rules.

This general standard of care was explained in *Nettleship* v *Weston* (1971).

> ### Nettleship v Weston (1971)
> The defendant was receiving driving lessons from her neighbour. She crashed and the claimant injured his leg. The court decided that the standard of care expected of a motorist was that of the ordinary reasonable driver, and it was assumed that such a driver would have passed his or her driving test. It did not matter that the defendant was a learner. She had fallen below the standard of care expected.

The standard of care expected can vary in different cases.

When using the objective test the court takes certain things into account, e.g. the defendant's age and profession, the characteristics of the claimant, and how dangerous the situation is.

1 The defendant's age

A young person will not have to reach the standard of care expected of an adult. The standard would be of the ordinary reasonable 12-year-old (for example).

> ### Mullin v Richards (1998)
> Two 15-year-old schoolgirls were having a 'sword fight' with plastic rulers. One snapped and a piece of plastic went into the claimant's eye. The defendant had not breached her duty as nobody had realised that is was potentially dangerous.

2 The defendant's profession

A doctor is expected to reach the standard required of a person at his or her level in the profession. He or she would not be expected to reach the standard of a specialist when he or she is only a junior doctor. Instead, the doctor would need to reach the standard of the ordinary reasonable junior doctor. This was established in *Bolam* v *Friern Hospital Management Committee* (1957).

> ### Bolam v Friern Hospital Management Committee (1957)
> When the court has to decide if a doctor has been negligent it will hear evidence from other doctors as to their thoughts of what is appropriate practice. This case involved a patient being injured after having electric shock treatment without a relaxant. The court decided that this was not negligent as

some doctors did use a relaxant drug and others did not. Whether a doctor has been a consultant for 1 day or 1 year does not affect the fact that he or she must reach the standard of care of the ordinary reasonable consultant. This was reaffirmed in *Djemal* v *Bexley Heath Health Authority* (1995).

3 Characteristics of the claimant

If the claimant is at more risk than usual of being harmed, then the defendant owes a higher standard of care to take extra precautions.

Paris v *Stepney Borough Council* (1951)

The claimant was blinded at work. He was able to claim compensation from his employer for not providing him with safety goggles. The defendants argued that the vehicle maintenance work that was being undertaken by the claimant was not dangerous enough to require goggles. The court decided that the defendants had fallen below the standard of care required, as they owed a higher standard to an employee who was more at risk. Paris was more at risk as he was already blind in one eye before the accident.

4 Magnitude of the risk

This is a landmark case.

Bolton v *Stone* (1951)

A ball that had been hit out of a cricket ground hit the claimant. This was a rare occurrence and the cricket club had built a high fence to try to prevent this from happening. The court decided that the defendants were not negligent as the likelihood of the risk was very low and people cannot be expected to prevent all accidents.

5 Whether the defendant has taken reasonable precautions

Latimer v *AEC Ltd* (1952)

The defendants owned a factory that had been flooded by heavy rain. The floor had become slippery with oil. The defendants had covered most of the floor with sawdust. The claimant slipped on an area without sawdust, even though it was clearly marked. The defendants were not negligent, as they had taken reasonable precautions.

6 Benefits of the risk

Watt v *Hertfordshire County Council* (1954)

The fire brigade transported equipment on an inappropriate fire engine to save a person trapped under a car. The fire engine that should have been used was out attending to another emergency. The equipment fell off the fire engine and injured the claimant. The defendant was not liable as the risk of injury was outweighed by the need to transport the equipment.

C Damage

The final element required to prove negligence is damage. There must be some sort of damage, e.g. personal injury or damage to property. If a motorist (duty of care) falls below the standard of care expected of the ordinary reasonable driver (breach of duty) but does no damage to anyone or anything, then he or she is not negligent.

In order to prove damage, the negligent act must have caused the damage and the type of damage must be foreseeable.

1 Causation

These are the same rules of causation used in criminal law.

The court must establish that the breach of duty caused the damage. To do this it uses the 'but for' test: would the claimant have suffered damage regardless of the defendant's act or omission?

> **Barnett v Chelsea and Kensington Hospital Management Committee (1968)**
> Three night watchmen had become sick from drinking tea. The hospital they attended telephoned a doctor and described the symptoms. The doctor did not know they had arsenic poisoning and told them to go home. Evidence showed that the doctor did not cause their death by not examining them, as they would have died anyway.

In some cases it can be difficult to establish what caused the claimant's damage.

This case involves multiple causes.

> **Wilsher v Essex Area Health Authority (1988)**
> The claimant had gone blind. Medical evidence showed that there were six possible causes of the blindness. The doctor's negligence had only been one of the possible causes, therefore the doctor was not negligent.

2 Remoteness of damage

This Australian case was decided by the Privy Council but has since been fully incorporated into the law of England and Wales.

The claimant must prove that the type of damage suffered was reasonably foreseeable. It is not enough to prove that any damage is foreseeable; it must be proved that the type of damage suffered is foreseeable. This was established in the case of *Wagon Mound* (1961).

> **Wagon Mound (1961)**
> A negligent oil spill from the defendant's tanker floated into Sydney Harbour. Sparks from welding ignited some of the oil and it set fire to the wharf. The defendant was not liable as this type of damage was not foreseeable.

Summary of Topic 18

In order to prove negligence, three things must be established: duty of care, breach of duty and damage.

Duty of care

The neighbour principle, established by Lord Atkin in *Donoghue* v *Stevenson* (1932) House of Lords, was the traditional way in which the court decided if a duty of care was owed. If a person was 'so closely and directly affected by your acts or omission' then you owed a duty of care.

The modern test was defined in *Caparo Industries plc* v *Dickman* (1990):
1 **Was the damage reasonably foreseeable?** Foresight of consequences is necessary. If the 'ordinary reasonable man' could not foresee the damage to the defendant, then a duty of care is not owed (*Bourhill* v *Young*, 1943, *Maguire* v *Harland and Wolff plc*, 2005).
2 **Was there sufficient proximity between the claimant and the defendant?** Proximity requires that the claimant and defendant have a legal connection. This link can either be a physical connection (*Donoghue* v *Stevenson*, 1932) or a relationship (*McLoughlin* v *O'Brian*, 1983).
3 **Is it just and fair to impose a duty of care?** *Griffiths* v *Lindsay* (1998).

Breach of duty

The standard of care required is described as a general standard. Breach of duty is established using the objective test (the standard of the ordinary reasonable man, or ordinary reasonable doctor).

This general standard of care was explained in *Nettleship* v *Weston* (1971).
1 **The defendant's age:** a young person will not have to reach the standard of care expected of an adult (*Mullin* v *Richards*, 1998).
2 **The defendant's profession:** a doctor is expected to reach the standard required of a person at his or her level in the profession (*Bolam* v *Friern Hospital Management Committee*, 1957).
3 **Characteristics of the claimant:** if the claimant is at more risk of being harmed, then the defendant owes a higher standard of care to take extra precautions (*Paris* v *Stepney Borough Council*, 1951).
4 **Magnitude of the risk:** *Bolton* v *Stone* (1951).
5 **Whether the defendant has taken reasonable precautions:** *Latimer* v *AEC Ltd* (1952).
6 **Benefits of the risk:** *Watt* v *Hertfordshire County Council* (1954).

Damage

1 **Causation:** 'but for' test — would the claimant have died anyway? (*Barnett* v *Chelsea and Kensington Hospital Management Committee*, 1968). There may be multiple causes (*Wilsher* v *Essex Area Health Authority*, 1988).
2 **Remoteness of damage:** the claimant must prove that the type of damage suffered was reasonably foreseeable (*Wagon Mound*, 1961).

Civil law should not seek to find people guilty and punish them; instead it is concerned with finding a remedy. This is a way to solve a dispute between the parties involved. If a motorist is negligent and crashes into another car, the owner of that car would want damages (money). If a person is constantly being disturbed by a neighbour's loud music, he or she may want an injunction (a court order).

A Damages

The aim of awarding a person damages is usually to compensate him or her. This means to put the person back in the position he or she was in before the tort had been committed. For example, if a motorist has negligently caused £1,000 worth of damage to your car, compensatory damages would award you that amount. Sometimes the courts award more damages (aggravated damages and exemplary damages) or less damages (contemptuous damages).

Compensatory damages

This is the most common remedy sought in a civil case. When calculating the amount of compensation, the judge considers two types of damages: general damages and special damages.

1.1 General damages

These are damages for injury and losses where it is difficult to give an exact price. They are also known as non-pecuniary losses. There are tariff guidelines issued by the Court of Appeal for the amount of compensation that a person suffering from different injuries can claim, but the amount of compensation varies with different circumstances.

Pain and suffering is difficult for the courts to compensate. Such claims can only be made for the time that the claimant could appreciate the pain and suffering. For example, a person cannot claim pain and suffering for the time that they have spent in a coma.

> ### *Hicks v South Yorkshire Police* (1992)
> Compensation for pain and suffering was not awarded to the victims of the Hillsborough disaster who were killed. The court decided that their deaths were very quick.

General damages also compensate loss of amenity, such as an inability to play sport after a person's injury, impaired senses or impaired sexual enjoyment. Loss of amenity differs from pain and suffering in that it can be claimed while the claimant is unaware of the loss (e.g. when the person is in a coma).

> ### *West and Son v Shephard* (1964)
> A claimant who was left partially unconscious and paralysed was awarded £17,500 for loss of amenity. She was unable to communicate but there

Claimants suffering whiplash from a car accident usually receive a standard amount of compensation.

was medical evidence to suggest that she had some appreciation of her circumstances.

Loss of future earnings is particularly difficult to calculate. The courts have to guess how long the claimant would have worked if he or she had not been injured and whether the claimant would have been promoted or made unemployed etc. The damages are awarded as a lump sum that, when invested as an annuity, will give the claimant an income for life or for the duration that the injury is likely to last. The claimant's net annual loss is the difference between his or her income before the injury and the income (if any) that he or she gets afterwards. Some claimants will not be able to work at all, whereas some may be able to work in a lower-paid job. The **multiplicand** is the amount that the court thinks the claimant's earnings would have altered, e.g. through promotion or changing job. The **multiplier** is a calculation of the amount of money required to invest that will give the annual income that the claimant is entitled to. With these two amounts the loss of earnings can be calculated.

> Multiplicand x multiplier = loss of earnings compensation.

Doyle v *Wallace* (1998)

The claimant was unable to work after a car accident. She was going to train to be a teacher but if she did not pass the exams she planned to do clerical work. The court estimated that she had a 50% chance of becoming a teacher. It awarded her loss of earnings that was halfway between what she would have earned in clerical work and what she would have earned as a teacher.

Fatal accidents are calculated using the **Fatal Accidents Act 1976**. Dependants can claim for financial losses that they have incurred from the claimant's death. The defendant may have to compensate the deceased's dependants.

Martin and Brown v *Grey* (1998)

The 12-year-old daughter of a woman who was killed was awarded compensation to provide the services of a mother.

1.2 Special damages

> Pecuniary means money.

These are damages that the courts are able to calculate exactly (also known as pecuniary losses). Special damages include loss of earnings up to the date of the trial, medical expenses, damage to property and any other loss that the claimant may have incurred.

When property is destroyed the claimant receives its market value.

2 Aggravated damages

The amount of damages awarded may be increased if the defendant has aggravated the claimant's injuries. According to Lord Devlin in *Rookes* v *Barnard* (1964), this includes humiliating the claimant or acting out of spite.

Ansell v *Thomas* (1974)

The claimant received aggravated damages when the police humiliated him when they wrongfully dragged him out of his business in front of his employees.

Such an award is criticised, as the civil law should not seek to punish.

Exemplary damages are also supposed to make an example of the loser and serve as a deterrent to others who may be considering doing the same.

The Law Commission Report 1997 recommended that the rule on exemplary damages should apply to all types of tort. In the case of *Kuddus* v *Chief Constable of Leicestershire Constabulary*, (2001) the House of Lords had the same view.

3

Exemplary damages

Exemplary damages are punitive. They seek to punish the loser in a civil case by awarding the winner more damages than are necessary to compensate them.

Cassell v *Broome* (1972)
The defendant made a libellous comment in his book about the claimant being a coward in the Second World War. The defendant calculated that he would still make a profit out of the book even after he had compensated the claimant. The courts saw this as behaviour that should not be encouraged. They therefore made the defendant pay exemplary damages so that he did not profit from his tort.

Rookes v *Barnard* (1964)
The House of Lords stated that exemplary damages may be awarded when:
- a statute allows such an award
- the defendant calculated that he or she would still make a profit after compensating the claimant (as in *Cassell* v *Broome*, 1972)
- a government official acted oppressively (as in *Russell McName and McCotter* v *Home Office*, 2001, where prison officers beat up an IRA prisoner who had escaped from prison)

4

Contemptuous damages

The court may show disapproval of a claimant's decision to take a case to court in the first place. If the judge believes that the case should never have made it to the court, the winner may be awarded contemptuous damages.

Pamplin v *Express Newspapers Ltd* (1988)
The claimant sued the *Daily Express* for defamation when the newspaper called him 'sleazy'. Pamplin had avoided paying parking tickets by registering his car in the name of his infant son. Although the court found in favour of Pamplin, the judge only awarded him the lowest coin of the Realm, which in 1988 was $\frac{1}{2}$p.

Equity is when cases are decided according to what is fair for both parties, rather that the judge following strict legal rules.

B Injunctions

The claimant in a civil case may want a court order that either forces the defendant to stop a certain activity or to make him or her do something. In the tort of nuisance, injunctions are a common remedy. If a neighbour is causing a nuisance by playing music too loudly, an injunction may stop him or her from playing it at certain times of day. However, if a neighbour's trees are blocking the sunlight to other houses, an injunction could force him or her to prune the trees.

The court will not grant an injunction if damages would be more appropriate. The court may also award damages as well as an injunction. An injunction will only be granted when it is equitable (fair) to do so. Courts will not make an injunction for trivial matters.

> *Llandudno UDC v Woods* (1899)
> The court refused to grant an injunction to stop people preaching on the beach as it was regarded as a trivial matter.

1 *Types of injunctions*

There are different types of injunction: mandatory, prohibitory and interim.

1.1 Mandatory injunction

This type of injunction forces the defendant to do something, e.g. prune a tree.

1.2 Prohibitory injunction

This type of injunction prevents the defendant from committing a tort, e.g. stop playing music.

1.3 Interim injunction

This type of injunction will be granted before the trial in the time leading up to when the judge will consider the case fully.

Injunctions can also be full or partial.

1.4 Full injunction

A full injunction prevents the defendant from committing the tort again.

1.5 Partial injunction

A partial injunction allows the defendant to commit the tort in certain circumstances.

> *Kennaway v Thompson* (1980)
> The claimant complained that a motorboat club was causing a nuisance to her lakeside property. The court decided that the noise from the boat club meetings and competitions was a nuisance and limited the club's activities instead of stopping them altogether.

Summary of Topic 19

Damages

The aim of awarding a person damages is usually to compensate him or her. This means to put the person back in the position that he or she was in before the tort had been committed.

1 **Compensatory damages:** when calculating the amount of compensation, the judge considers two types of damages:

   a **General damages** are damages for injury and losses where it is difficult to give an exact price, e.g. pain and suffering (*Hicks* v *South Yorkshire Police*, 1992), loss of amenity (*West and Son* v *Shephard*, 1964), loss of future

earnings (multiplicand × multiplier = loss of earnings compensation) and fatal accidents when the dependants require compensation (*Martin and Brown v Grey*, 1998).

   b **Special damages** include loss of earnings up to the date of the trial, medical expenses, damage to property and any other loss that the claimant may have incurred.

2 **Aggravated damages:** the amount of damages awarded may be increased if the defendant has aggravated the claimant's injuries. According to Lord Devlin in *Rookes v Barnard* (1964), this includes humiliating the claimant or acting out of spite, e.g. *Ansell v Thomas* (1974).

3 **Exemplary damages:** these seek to punish the loser in a civil case by awarding the winner more damages than are necessary to compensate them, e.g. *Cassell v Broome* (1972) and *Rookes v Barnard* (1964).

4 **Contemptuous damages:** these show the court's disapproval of a claimant's decision to take a case to court in the first place, e.g. *Pamplin v Express Newspapers Ltd* (1988).

Injunctions

The court will not grant an injunction if damages would be more appropriate. The court may also award damages as well as an injunction. An injunction will only be granted when it is equitable (fair) to do so. Courts will not make an injunction for trivial matters, e.g. *Llandudno UDC v Woods* (1899). There are several different types of injunction:

1 **Mandatory injunction:** this forces the defendant to do something.

2 **Prohibitory injunction:** this prevents the defendant from committing a tort.

3 **Interim injunction:** this is granted before the trial in the time leading up to when the judge considers the case fully.

4 **Full injunction:** this prevents the defendant from committing the tort again.

5 **Partial injunction:** this allows the defendant to commit the tort in certain circumstances, e.g. *Kennaway v Thompson* (1980).